STARK

A Practitioner's Guide

DONALD H. ROMANO

AMERICAN BAR ASSOCIATION
Health Law Section

Cover design by Mary Anne Kulchawik/ABA Design

Printed in the United States of America.

27 26 25 24 23   5 4 3 2 1

Library of Congress Cataloging-in-Publication Data

Names: Romano, Donald H., author.
Title: Stark : a practitioner's guide / Donald H. Romano.
Description: Chicago, Illinois : ABA Publishing, American Bar Association, [2023] | Includes bibliographical references and index. | Summary: "This book presents a comprehensive examination of the Stark Law and its implementing regulations. Contrary to the belief of some, Stark is not rocket science, but there are a lot of nooks and crannies of which practitioners need to be aware in order to practice competently in this area. Although the book delves into considerable detail in some areas, there are many more weeds to wade through that I walked around"-- Provided by publisher.
Identifiers: LCCN 2023017800 (print) | LCCN 2023017801 (ebook) | ISBN 9781639053575 (hardcover) | ISBN 9781639053582 (epub)
Subjects: LCSH: Medical referral--Law and legislation--United States. | Medical laws and legislation--United States. | Medicare--Law and legislation. | Medicaid--Law and legislation.
Classification: LCC KF2907.P38 R66 2023 (print) | LCC KF2907.P38 (ebook) | DDC 344.7304/1--dc23/eng/20230712
LC record available at https://lccn.loc.gov/2023017800
LC ebook record available at https://lccn.loc.gov/2023017801

Contents

Acknowledgments

The author is grateful to those who submitted comments on a draft version of this book, particularly Hayden Wool and Larry Vernaglia.

About the Author

Donald H. Romano counsels clients on regulatory compliance matters, particularly those pertaining to the Anti-Kickback Statute, the physician self-referral statute (Stark Law), HIPAA, and the Medicare enrollment regulations. He also advises hospitals and other providers and suppliers on Medicare reimbursement issues. Prior to practicing on his own, Mr. Romano was Of Counsel in the Washington, D.C. office of Foley & Lardner LLP. Prior to joining Foley, Mr. Romano was a partner in another D.C.-based law firm, and prior to that he had over 25 years of experience in the Department of Health and Human Services, including as a senior attorney in the Office of General Counsel, and as a Division Director in the Centers for Medicare & Medicaid Services. In that latter position, he was responsible for, among other things, Stark policy, Provider Reimbursement Review Board procedures, and the Anti-Markup Rule.

Mr. Romano is a frequent speaker and author on health law topics. He is a past officer of the the American Bar Association Health Law Section and a past chair of that Section's Interest Group on Fraud and Compliance, as well as a past vice-chair of the American Health Lawyers Association's Regulations, Accreditation and Payment Group. He is a recipient of the Secretary's Distinguished Service Award (the highest individual service award from HHS), the Patricia Meador Leadership Award (given by the Fraud and Compliance Section of the American Health Lawyers Association), and a Burton Award (national writing award), and is listed in multiple editions of The Best Lawyers in America. He earned his J.D. from the University of Baltimore in 1984 and his B.A. from Towson University. He is admitted to the bars of the District of Columbia, Maryland, and Massachusetts.

Author's Note

This book presents a comprehensive examination of the Stark Law and its implementing regulations.[1] Contrary to the belief of some, Stark is not rocket science, but there are a lot of nooks and crannies of which practitioners need to be aware in order to practice competently in this area. Although the book delves into considerable detail in some areas, there are many more weeds to wade through that I walked around. The reader will note that there are, naturally, some points of CMS policy (comparatively, not many) with which I disagree. The reader must make up his or her mind as to these points, and others, and what action to take. For example, the reader may not agree with some view expressed in a preamble to a final rule and must decide, within the bounds of legally permissible options, whether to advise his or her client to conform a proposed or ongoing arrangement to CMS's view or to his or her view, and if the

[1] Many of the states have their own version of a physician or practitioner self-referral law. They are not discussed in this book. Note that some of the state self-referral laws pertain to ownership/investment interests only, some pertain to a limited type of services only, and some have exceptions that mirror some of the Stark exceptions. In other words, there is a great deal of variety among such laws. Practitioners should familiarize themselves with the relevant state law or laws, if any, when analyzing an arrangement for Stark compliance. Likewise, this book does not discuss the Federal Anti-Kickback Statute (AKS), section 1128B(b) of the Social Security Act, 42 U.S.C. § 1320a-7b(b), or any state "all-payor" anti-kickback statute. Some arrangements that are compliant under Stark may not be so under the AKS, or vice versa.

arrangement has already commenced or terminated whether there is a duty to self-disclose.

Although I have attempted to proceed in an orderly fashion, there are certain concepts and principles that can appear in more than one aspect of a Stark analysis. Thus, there is some material that is repeated one or more times out of concern that it might otherwise escape the practitioner's attention when conducting a Stark analysis. Also, an index is included at the end of the book to help in this regard.

Whereas more emphasis is given to the current state of the Stark regulations and CMS policy, the reader should bear in mind that previous versions of the regulations and interpretations may be relevant or determinative of the Stark compliance of an existing arrangement. An arrangement that was previously compliant may now be noncompliant due to a change in the regulations,[2] or vice versa.[3] In either case, the practitioner would need to take into account the rules in effect during all periods of the subject arrangement, whether referrals for DHS were made during such periods, and whether a self-disclosure is required with respect to some, all, or none of the periods of the arrangement.

As a reminder this book presents the author's views and is not intended as legal advice. This book is current through June 2023.

---

[2] For example, the 2020 final rule now requires, for purposes of certain exceptions, directed referral arrangements meet specified criteria. Previously, meeting such criteria served only as a safe harbor to guard against a claim that the directed referral arrangement impermissibly took into account the volume or value of referrals or other business generated.

[3] For example, the 2020 final rule provides that parties to an arrangement protected by an exception that requires a year term now may modify the compensation terms mid-arrangement without extending the termination date, but previously the parties to such an arrangement would have been required to extend the termination date to at least a year from the effective date of the modification.

1
Introduction to the Stark Law

OUTLINE

A. Basic Prohibitions and Statutory Background

The Physician Self-Referral Law,[1] commonly known as the Stark Law, prohibits a physician from referring Medicare patients for certain services known as designated health services (DHS) to an entity with which the physician or an immediate family member of the physician has a direct or indirect financial relationship. The

[1] Section 1877 of the Social Security Act, 42 U.S.C. § 1395nn.

law also prohibits an entity, such as a hospital or other provider or supplier, from billing Medicare (or any other payor) for DHS furnished as a result of a prohibited referral. Notwithstanding the above prohibitions, there are a number of statutory and additional regulatory exceptions that, if applicable and satisfied, protect the financial relationship or protect the referral at issue. Thus, for analysis purposes, the basic formulation of the law may be stated thus: If a physician (or his or her immediate family member) has a financial relationship with an entity (e.g., s/he rents office space from a hospital), the physician may not refer a patient for DHS to such entity, and the entity may not bill for such services, unless an exception (or waiver) is satisfied.

The law was enacted in 1989[2] and named after then–California Congressman Fortney Hillman "Pete" Stark, Jr. The purpose of the law was to address the perceived problem of physician self-referrals, which Congress described as the practice of a physician referring Medicare clinical laboratory business to an entity with which the physician (or his or her immediate family member) has a financial relationship. Congress's concern, in its most basic form, was that a physician who self-refers might overuse items and services paid for by Medicare to further his or her own financial interest, leading to both increased costs to the federal health care system and adverse impacts on patient care. The original version of the law (which is known as Stark I) applied to self-referral of clinical lab services only. In 1993, the law was broadened to cover self-referral of 10 additional services.[3] These services are referred to in the law and regulations as designated health services, or DHS.

The Stark Law is a strict liability law, which means that no intent to violate the statute is necessary for claims for DHS to be denied or a violation to be found. In addition, however, there are enhanced penalties for *knowing* violations. As such, whenever an arrangement involves a financial relationship with a physician who refers DHS

---

[2] Section 6204 of the Omnibus Budget Reconciliation Act of 1989, Pub. L. No. 101–239, 103 STAT 2106.

[3] Section 13562 of the Omnibus Budget Reconciliation Act of 1993, Pub. L. No. 101-203, 107 STAT 312. The law was also amended in 1990 and 1994, in minor ways. *See* 60 Fed. Reg. at 41915 (the 1995 Stark I final rule) for a discussion of these amendments.

that are payable by Medicare, the proposed arrangement must be evaluated for compliance with the Stark Law based on the specific facts and circumstances.

B. Regulatory History

The Secretary of Health and Human Service (HHS) is responsible for administering Title XVIII (also called the Medicare Statute) of the Social Security Act. The Secretary delegated to the Centers for Medicare & Medicaid Services (CMS), an agency within HHS, responsibility for interpreting the Stark Law and issuing regulations and other guidance.[4] Through its oversight of the law, CMS has published a series of proposed and final regulations that implement and attempt to explain Stark (the "Stark Regulations"). The Stark Regulations both implement the statutory exceptions and, pursuant to statutory authority,[5] set forth additional exceptions.

The statutory text of the Stark Law is only the beginning of the law's implementation, interpretation, and enforcement. The Stark Regulations are the lifeblood of the statute and play the largest role in informing the health care industry of its requirements. Therefore, in order to advise clients that propose to enter into arrangements in which DHS will be referred by physicians to entities with which they have a financial relationship, one cannot simply consult the statute but instead must have a thorough knowledge of the regulations.

The Stark Regulations are found at 42 C.F.R. §§ 411.350–411.389. The regulations define terms, describe various types of financial relationships, set forth the requirements of the exceptions, describe how to request an advisory opinion, and present other related matters.

---

4 The delegation was actually made to the Health Care Financing Administration (HCFA), the predecessor in name to CMS. For ease of reference, "CMS" will be used instead of "HCFA," even when historically inaccurate.

5 Section 1877(b)(4) of the Social Security Act, 42 U.S.C. § 1395nn(b)(4) authorizes the Secretary to promulgate new exceptions that do not create a risk of program or patient abuse. CMS interprets its statutory authority as allowing it to expand additional statutory exceptions as well as permitting it to create entirely new exceptions.

The discussion in this chapter focuses on the history of the various rulemakings that make up the Stark Regulations. It is important to familiarize oneself with the rulemakings, especially the more significant ones,[6] in order to know where to look for CMS's thoughts and analysis of various terms, concepts, exceptions, etc. It is important to keep in mind that, occasionally, a certain policy or interpretation expressed in one rulemaking may have been altered or reversed in a subsequent rulemaking. What follows is a fairly comprehensive itemization of the topics covered in selected rulemakings. The reader is cautioned that the rulemakings discussed in this chapter, and the topics within the rulemakings, are only the more prominent ones.[7] The descriptions of the topics are necessarily brief, and therefore, the actual rulemakings must be consulted to get a full and accurate story.[8] Succeeding chapters of this book cover the content of the regulations, but by necessity this book cannot address every point of discussion in the preambles of the proposed and final rules. Practitioners are implored to consult the preambles when performing a Stark analysis.

1. Stark I Final Regulations

The first round of Stark Regulations was promulgated in connection with the original 1989 Stark Law (Stark I), which applied to clinical laboratory services only. The proposed rule was published in 1992,[9] and the final rule was published on August 14, 1995,[10] after Stark II, the expanded Stark Law, was enacted as part of the Omnibus

[6] Although all of the various rulemakings have some degree of importance, in the author's estimation the most important rulemakings are (in chronological order): the 1998 proposed rule; the Phase I, Phase II, and Phase III final rules; the FY 2009 IPPS final rule; the CY 2016 PFS final rule, and the 2020 final rule.

[7] Note that an almost complete listing, in reverse chronological order, of the Stark rulemakings appears on CMS's website at https://www.cms.gov/Medicare/Fraud-and-Abuse/PhysicianSelfReferral/Significant-Regulatory-History.

[8] CMS maintains a complete list of the Stark rulemakings, which can be found at https://www.cms.gov/Medicare/Fraud-and-Abuse/PhysicianSelfReferral/Significant-Regulatory-History. Of course, the practitioner should keep in mind that there may be some lag time between recently published rulemakings and their appearance on CMS's website.

[9] 57 Fed. Reg. 8588 (Mar. 11, 1992).

[10] 60 Fed. Reg. 41914 (Aug. 14, 1995).

Budget Reconciliation Act (OBRA) of 1993. Notwithstanding the two-year lag between the enactment of Stark II and the 1995 final rule, the final rule was intended to "address only those provisions of section 1877 that are effective as of January 1, 1992."[11] In other words, the 1995 final rule applied to referrals for clinical laboratory services only. However, CMS stated in the 1995 final rule that it believed that a majority of its interpretations in the 1995 final rule would apply to the expanded list of DHS, and that, until it published further rulemaking, it intended to rely on language and interpretations in the 1995 final rule with respect to referrals for any DHS.[12] Thus, the 1995 final rule remains relevant and provides authoritative guidance for some areas of Stark.

2. Stark II, Phase I Regulations[13]

Following a comprehensive proposed rule in 1998,[14] the first round of regulations under Stark II was issued on January 4, 2001 (known as the Phase I final rule). The Phase I final rule did not take effect, for the most part, until a year later, on January 4, 2002. The Phase I final rule addressed the general statutory broadening of Stark to cover 10 additional DHS as opposed to the limited application (clinical laboratory services only) of the first regulations from 1995. The Phase I final rule addressed the general prohibition on self-referrals, and also began the discussion of the service-based exceptions that apply to both ownership or investment interests and compensation arrangements (e.g., the in-office ancillary services exception). However, the Phase I final rule purposefully did not address all the areas covered by the 1998 proposed rule because future rounds of rulemaking were already anticipated. Overall, the Phase I final rule with comment period took a more industry-friendly approach in several respects as

---

11 *See* 60 Fed. Reg. at 41916.

12 *Id.*

13 66 Fed. Reg. 856 (Jan. 4, 2001).

14 63 Fed. Reg. 1659 (Jan. 9, 1998). Although certain proposed positions in the 1998 proposed rule were rejected by the 2001 Phase I final rule, as discussed below, the 1998 proposed rule remains an important source for interpreting the Stark Law.

compared to what was proposed in the 1998 proposed rule.[15] In the Phase I final rule CMS expressed its philosophical approach to the Stark Law, which, with perhaps a few departures, has been consistent throughout the years. It said:

> First, we have tried in Phase I of this rulemaking to interpret the prohibitions narrowly and the exceptions broadly, to the extent consistent with the statutory language and intent. As a practical matter, we believe that, while the statute must be implemented to achieve its intent, we should be cautious in interpreting its reach so broadly as to prohibit potentially beneficial financial arrangements.[16]

The final rule also made clarifications and changes to certain defined terms, such as "employee," "entity," "fair market value," "immediate family member," and "remuneration."[17] One of the most important changes in Phase I was defining "referral" to exclude personally performed services.[18]

The Phase I final rule established several new exceptions,[19] namely, exceptions for: indirect compensation arrangements; fair market value arrangements; nonmonetary compensation; risk sharing

---

15 The ABA Health Law Section published a detailed overview of the Phase I Regulations in a special edition of THE HEALTH LAWYER in January 2001. The edition, entitled "Stark II Final Rule—Phase I: A Kinder and Gentler Stark?" describes all aspects of the Phase I final rule in detail.

16 *See* 66 Fed. Reg. at 860. CMS further stated that, as a corollary to this approach, it believed that Congress intended the Stark Law to establish only "a minimum threshold for acceptable financial relationships, and that potentially abusive financial relationships that may be permitted under [the Stark Law] could still be addressed through other statutes that address health care fraud and abuse, including the anti-kickback statute." *Id.* It then stated that a third consideration in developing the Phase I final rule was to not adversely affect medical care for federal health care beneficiaries and other patients. *Id.*

17 *See id.* at 942-49.

18 *See id.* at 871-72.

19 Section 1877(b)(4) of the Social Security Act, 42 U.S.C. § 1395nn(b)(4), authorizes the Secretary of HHS to create additional exceptions, or expand existing exceptions, where doing so does not pose a risk of program or patient abuse.

arrangements; compliance training programs; medical staff benefits; academic medical centers; implants in an ambulatory surgical center (ASC); erythropoietin (EPO) and other dialysis related drugs; preventive screening tests, immunizations, and vaccines; and eyeglasses and contact lenses.

The final rule provides extensive guidance on the in-office ancillary services (IOAS) exception[20] and the closely related topic of the definition of "group practice."[21]

With respect to the IOAS exception, CMS established that the degree of supervision for purposes of the exception is whatever the Medicare payment rules require for the particular diagnostic test at issue. Thus, if the payment rules require only general supervision, the level of supervision for the IOAS exception is general. This policy is notable because the statutory IOAS exception uses the language "directly supervised,"[22] and the 1995 Stark I final rule, and the 1998 proposed rule took that to mean "direct supervision."[23]

In its guidance on the definition of "group practice" CMS made clear that its overarching view of Congressional intent is that referrals for DHS within a "group practice" should be protected only if the group practice is a bona fide group practice and not a loose confederation of individual physicians bound together primarily to profit from DHS referrals. On the other hand, CMS stated, if the group was truly integrated, it did not believe that Congress otherwise intended to regulate the formal structure and operation of the group.[24] Among other things, the Phase I final rule excluded independent contractors from the definition of a "member" of a group practice, but also provided that independent contractors may qualify as "physicians in the group practice,"[25] and that such physicians could receive profit shares and productivity bonuses to the same extent as members of the group.[26]

---

[20] *See id.* at 880-894.
[21] *See id.* at 894-911.
[22] *See* section 1877(b)(2)(A)(i) of the Social Security Act, 42 U.S.C. 1395nn(b)(2)(A)(i).
[23] *See* 63 Fed. Reg. at 1666.
[24] *See* 66 Fed. Reg. at 895.
[25] *See id.* at 899-900.
[26] *See id.* at 899-909.

Importantly, the Phase I final rule set forth the test—which continued in effect until the effective date of the 2020 final rule—of what does *not* take into account the volume or value of referrals or other business. It said that

> A compensation arrangement does not take into account the volume or value of referrals or other business generated between the parties if the compensation is fixed in advance and will result in fair market value compensation, and the compensation does not vary over the term of the arrangement in any manner that takes into account referrals or other business generated.[27]

This policy was incorporated into the "special rules on compensation" at section 411.354(d) for per unit ("per click") compensation.[28]

Finally, the Phase I final rule also instituted CMS's practice of publishing in the Federal Register a list of Current Procedural Terminology (CPT) and Health Care Financing Administration (HCFA) Common Procedure Coding System (HCPCS) codes that are DHS, for certain categories of DHS.[29]

3. Stark II, Phase II Regulations[30]

The second round of regulations under Stark II was issued on March 26, 2004 (the Phase II Regulations). The Phase II Regulations, which became effective on July 26, 2004, responded to numerous comments received in connection with the 1998 proposed rule by broadening or revising some exceptions and creating additional exceptions. The Phase II Regulations were an attempt to reduce the regulatory

---

27 *See id.* at 877-78.

28 At this time, percentage compensation was not considered to be "set in advance." As noted below, that would change with the Phase II final rule, but in the Phase III final rule CMS declined, without explanation, to incorporate percentage compensation into the special rules on compensation.

29 *See* 66 Fed. Reg. at 922-42. The list is updated yearly and appears on CMS's website at https://www.cms.gov/medicare/fraud-and-abuse/physicianselfreferral/list_of_codes.

30 69 Fed. Reg. 16054 (Mar. 26, 2004).

burdens on the health care industry by easing some of the restrictions from the Phase I Regulations.[31]

The Phase II final rule created new exceptions for temporary noncompliance (§ 411.353(f)), intra-family referrals (§ 411.355(j)), charitable donations by a physician (§ 411.357(j)) referral services (§ 411.357(q)), obstetrical malpractice insurance subsidies (§ 411.357(r)), retention payments made to physicians in an underserved area (§ 411.357(t)), and community-wide health systems (§ 411.357(u)).

The rule also made modifications and clarifications to several exceptions.

CMS stated that the whole hospital exception protects referrals to the hospital only—it does not protect referrals to entities that are owned by a hospital.[32] The final rule amended the lease exceptions to allow terminations, with or without cause, provided that no further agreement is entered into within the first year of the original term, and allowed holdovers for up to six months, provided that the arrangement continues on the same terms and conditions.[33] With respect to the exception for bona fide employee arrangements, it rejected the proposal in the 1998 proposed rule to prohibit productivity bonuses based on personally performed services.[34]

It modified the exception for personal service arrangements to provide for terminations to the same extent permitted under the lease exceptions. It also made a distinction between employees and independent contractors hired by a physician to perform the personal services.[35]

---

[31] The ABA Health Law Section again published a detailed overview of the Phase II Regulations in THE HEALTH LAWYER. The second overview, "Stark II—Phase II—The Final Voyage," was published in an April 2004 special edition.

[32] *See* 69 Fed. Reg. at 16084-85.

[33] *See id.* at 16085-86.

[34] *See id.* at 16086-89.

[35] CMS said:

> The commenter's proposal [to allow physicians to hire independent contractors] would present a potential for abuse. The personal service arrangements exception is not limited to professional services, and physicians may be hired to provide non-physician services as well. Allowing physicians to use independent contractors to provide services would allow a physician to enter into brokering arrangements for virtually any kind of service and take a fee as a middle person, without actually performing any services. This is contrary to the intent and purpose of the statute.

The Phase II final rule interpreted the exception for services unrelated to DHS narrowly. It found that the exception "is intended to be very limited and available only if the remuneration is wholly unrelated to the provision of DHS, such as the rental of residential property."[36]

The final rule expanded the statutory physician recruitment exception by allowing recruitment assistance payments to be made indirectly to a physician by way of a physician practice, clarified that the mileage for the relocation requirement is measured from the physician's existing practice and not the physician's residence, and provided that residents and physicians who have been in medical practice less than one year are exempted from the relocation requirement.[37]

A significant portion of the rule was devoted to responding to comments on the new exceptions promulgated by the Phase I final rule.[38]

Finally, the Phase II final rule contains a chart that shows, for various exceptions, (i) whether and to what extent physicians may be paid a profit share or productivity bonus, (ii) the scope of the volume/value prohibition, and (iii) whether the compensation must be fair market value or set in advance.[39]

> Using *bona fide* employees to provide contract services is different. The employment relationship ties the employee to the physician in a manner evidencing a *bona fide* business operated by the physician to provide the services. Along these same lines, we agree that a physician should be able to use a wholly owned company to provide contracted services under the exception.

Id. at 16090.

36 CMS reasoned that

> under the original statute, the exception was necessary to insulate a hospital's relationships with physicians that were unrelated to the provision of clinical laboratory services, a very small element of a hospital's practice. Since 1995, however, all hospital services are DHS and a narrower interpretation of the exception is required to prevent abuse. Given this breadth of DHS, the statute's purpose, and the industry's desire for bright line rules in connection with section 1877 of the Act, we will treat any item, service, or cost that could be allocated in whole or in part to Medicare or Medicaid under applicable cost reporting principles as related to the provision of DHS.

Id. at 16093.

37 *See id.* at 16094-97.

38 *See id.* at 16108-118.

39 *See id.* at 16067-68. The chart is misleading with respect to the scope of permitted productivity bonuses in the employment exception. The chart implies that productivity bonuses may be based only on personally performed services, but this is true only with respect to DHS. The exception does not prohibit productivity bonuses based on other business generated.

4. Stark II, Phase III Regulations[40]

The third round of major regulations under Stark II was issued on September 5, 2007 (the Phase III final rule). The Phase III final rule became effective on December 4, 2007, although certain applications of the stand-in-the-shoes rules were delayed by a subsequent, emergency rule published on November 15, 2007. The Phase III final rule responded to comments raised during the prior phases of the regulations and addressed the entirety of the Stark regulatory scheme then in effect.[41] CMS again stated that the latest regulations were designed to simplify requirements and provide flexibility to those in the health care industry.[42]

The final rule made changes to, and/or provided guidance on, certain definitions. It modified the definition of "physician in the group practice" to clarify that an independent contractor physician must furnish patient care services for the group under a contractual arrangement *directly* with the group practice, and provided other guidance concerning the definition;[43] removed the safe harbors from the definition of fair market value;[44] offered guidance on "incident to" services and clarified that diagnostic services cannot be furnished incident to a physician's service because diagnostic services have their own benefit category under Medicare;[45] and provided guidance on the definitions of "radiology and certain imaging services" and "referral" (including why CMS believes that durable medical equipment (DME) services will rarely be able to be personally performed by a physician and thus rarely will be able to escape being referrals).[46] The rule also provided extensive guidance of the definition of "group practice" with respect to productivity bonuses that take into account services performed incident to a physician's personally performed service.[47]

---

[40] 72 Fed. Reg. at 51012 (Sept. 5, 2007).

[41] The ABA Health Law Section published a third overview of the Stark Regulations at the time the Phase III regulations were finalized. The third overview, "Stark II Phase III—'The Full Picture,'" was published in a special edition of THE HEALTH LAWYER in September 2007.

[42] 73 Fed. Reg. at 51013.

[43] *See id.* at 51017-18.

[44] *See id.* at 51015-16.

[45] *See id.* at 51016-17.

[46] *See id.* at 51018-19, 51019-51021.

[47] See *id.* at 51021-24.

To the list of interests that are considered not to be ownership or investment interests, the rule added a security interest taken by a physician in equipment sold to a hospital and financed by a loan from the physician to the hospital.[48]

The Phase III final rule reiterated that percentage compensation arrangements can be considered "set in advance" but declined (without explanation) to amend the special rules on compensation at 411.354 (d)(2) and (d)(3) to make mention of percentage compensation arrangements.[49]

The Phase III final rule created no new exceptions, but made changes to several of the existing exceptions. It made extensive changes to the physician recruitment exception,[50] and provided an alternative route for satisfying the retention payments to a physician in an underserved area exception.[51] It also added holdover protection to the exception for personal services (which protection was already in the lease exceptions).

The final rule modified the exception for fair market compensation to provide that the exception may apply to compensation provided to an entity from a physician as well as compensation provided to a physician from an entity (previously only the latter was protected by the exception). It clarified that the exception is not applicable to leases for office space because the provision of space is neither an item nor a service, and clarified that the exception may not be used to protect physician recruitment arrangements because money spent on recruitment of physicians who will not be employed by the hospital offering the recruitment incentives is for the benefit of the community and not for services provided to the hospital.[52]

The final rule clarified that for purposes of the exception for charitable donations by a physician, donations may not be solicited or *offered* in any manner that reflects the volume or value of referrals.[53]

---

[48] *See id.* at 51027.
[49] *See id.* at 51031 (first column).
[50] *See id.* at 51047-54.
[51] *See id.* at 51065-68.
[52] *See id.* at 51059-60.
[53] *See id.* at 51057.

The final rule modified the exception for nonmonetary compensation by deeming nonmonetary compensation to be within the annual limit if the entity inadvertently exceeded the limit by no more than 50 percent during a calendar year and the physician repays the excess compensation within the earlier of the end of the calendar year or 180 days from the date the excess nonmonetary compensation was received. The final rule also modified the exception by providing that entities with a formal medical staff may provide one local medical staff appreciation event per year (which must be open to all medical staff), without having to count the entity's cost per medical staff member for such event against the annual limit.[54]

The final rule modified the exception for compliance training to permit compliance training programs that involve continuing medical education (CME) credit, provided that compliance training predominates.[55,56]

The final rule made changes to the exception for professional courtesy by clarifying that the exception applies only to hospitals and other providers with formal medical staffs, and by removing the requirement that that an entity notify an insurer where the professional courtesy involves the whole or partial reduction of any coinsurance obligation.[57] It provided guidance on the exception for indirect compensation arrangements.[58]

Finally, the rule reveals CMS's thinking as to why, as a practical matter, group practices that engage in shared facilities arrangements within the "same building," must do so through block leases.[59]

---

54 *See id.* at 51058-59.

55 *See id.* at 51061. Free or reduced cost CME is a subject that practitioners frequently encounter. The potential exceptions that may cover such CME are few and limited (e.g., the exception for non-monetary compensation). Note that, in a May 06, 2008, letter to the American Medical Association, CMS stated that "for purposes of our physician self-referral rules, we do not consider on-site CME to be remuneration if it is primarily for the benefit of the hospital's patients, for example, training on the prevention of nosocomial infection."

56 It would seem that other, i.e., non-CME, training could also be furnished, provided that compliance training predominates.

57 *See id.* at 51064-65.

58 *See id.* at 51061-63.

59 *See id.* at 51033.

5. FY 2009 IPPS Final Rule[60]

In the Fiscal Year 2009 Inpatient Prospective Payment System (IPPS) final rule, CMS made three significant changes to its regulations and several other noteworthy changes. First, it revised the "stand in the shoes" doctrine (which was issued in the Phase III final rule) to require only physician owners (true owners and not nominal owners) of a physician organization to stand in the shoes of the physician organization.[61] Second, it added to the definition of "entity" to provide that an entity also furnishes DHS if it performs services that are billed as DHS.[62] Third, it amended certain exceptions to remove from their protection percentage-based leases and certain "per click" leases.[63]

The rule also: issued safe harbors for when parties could know that the "period of disallowance" ended no later than the occurrence of certain events;[64] reversed the Phase III position that compensation terms of an arrangement may not be amended during the first year of the term;[65] revised the definition of "physician" and "physician organization";[66] promulgated a grace period for obtaining required signatures for purposes of meeting an exception;[67] revised the exception for malpractice insurance subsidies;[68] clarified the exclusion from the definition of "ownership or investment interest" for an interest in a retirement plan;[69] and placed the burden of persuasion on the claimant in any appeal of a denial of payment for a DHS that was made on the basis that the service was furnished pursuant to a prohibited referral.[70]

---

60 73 Fed. Reg. 38502 (July 7, 2008).

61 *See* 73 Fed. Reg. at 48693-699. The FY 2009 IPPS final rule did not adopt a proposed "entity stand in the shoes" doctrine. *See id.* at 48699.

62 *See id.* at 48721-39.

63 *See id.* at 48705-21.

64 *See id.* at 48700-05.

65 *See id.* at 48696-97.

66 *See id.* at 48700.

67 *See id.* at 48705-09.

68 *See id.* at 48735-37.

69 *See id.* at 48737-38.

70 *See id.* at 48738-40.

6. CY 2011 Outpatient Prospective Payment System (OPPS) Final Rule[71]

This rule contains CMS's initial and most comprehensive interpretation and discussion of the 2010 statutory changes to the whole hospital exception and the rural provider exception (as it applies to hospitals).[72] Of note is CMS's decree that the ownership or investment interests of non-referring physicians need not be considered when calculating the baseline physician ownership level,[73] a position that was later reversed in the 2016 PFS final rule (see below).

7. The CY 2016 Physician Fee Schedule (PFS) Final Rule[74]

In this rule, CMS issued two new compensation exceptions—one for assistance to compensate a non-physician practitioner (411.357(x))[75] and one for timeshare arrangements (411.357(y)).[76]

The rule also: liberalized the grace period rule for obtaining all necessary signatures, to include the situation where the failure to obtain such signatures was not inadvertent, from 30 days to 90 days;[77] stated that parties may use a collection of contemporaneous documents evidencing the course of conduct between them to satisfy the writing requirement of exceptions;[78] explained the difference between an "arrangement" and an "agreement" as those terms are used in the exceptions, and clarified that the one-year term requirement of certain exceptions may be satisfied if the arrangements lasts at least a year, even if the term of at least one year is not specified in the agreement.[79]

The rule also: amended the regulatory provisions regarding the public website and public advertising disclosure requirement imposed as part of the 2010 statutory changes to the whole hospital and rural

---

[71] 75 Fed. Reg. 71800 (Nov. 24, 2010).
[72] *See id.* at 72240-52.
[73] *See id.* at 72250.
[74] 80 Fed. Reg. 70886 (November 16, 2015).
[75] *See* 80 Fed. Reg. at 71301-11.
[76] *See id.* at 71325-33.
[77] *See id.* at 71333-34.
[78] *See id.* at 71315.
[79] *See id.* at 71317-18.

provider exceptions;[80] reversed its prior position on whether the ownership or investment interests of non-referring physicians must be included for purposes of the baseline physician ownership percentage for purposes of the whole hospital exception;[81] and amended the lease and personal service arrangements exceptions to allow for unlimited holdover period protection.[82]

8. The 2020 Final Rule[83]

The December 2, 2020, final rule (2020 final rule) was issued the same day as the Office of the Inspector General's (OIG's) final rule[84] adding and revising safe harbors under the Anti-Kickback Statute (AKS). The rules were issued pursuant to the Secretary's "Regulatory Sprint to Coordinated Care" initiative, and each is massive. Several of the Stark exceptions added by the 2020 final rule have corresponding new AKS safe harbors, so the rules should be read together (if one has the time and stamina). The final rule was generally effective for referrals for DHS made on or after January 19, 2021, but the provisions regarding changes to the "group practice" definition were effective for referrals for DHS on or after January 1, 2022.

The 2020 final rule added three exceptions for value-based arrangements,[85] an exception for limited remuneration to a physician[86] and an exception for cybersecurity technology and related services.[87] It created new definitions for compensation to a physician that takes into account the volume or value of referrals or other business generated, as well as corresponding definitions for compensation from a physician that takes into account the volume or value of referrals or other business generated. It left the special rules on compensation at 411.354(d)(2) and (3) in place, but added language that largely nullifies them.

---

80 *See id.* at 71335-37.
81 *See id.* at 71337-40.
82 *See id.* at 71318-20.
83 85 Fed. Reg. 77492 (Dec. 2, 2020).
84 85 Fed. Reg. 77684 (Dec. 2, 2020).
85 42 C.F.R. § 411.357(aa)(1), (2) and (3).
86 42 C.F.R. § 411.357(z).
87 42 C.F.R. § 411.357(bb).

The final rule created a definition for commercial reasonableness, which states in part that an arrangement may be commercially reasonable even if it does not result in profit for one or more of the parties. It simplified the definition for fair market value, and removed from the definition the concept of taking into account the volume or value of referrals. It repealed the safe harbors for knowing that the period of disallowance ends no later than a certain event, and commentary in the final rule evidences CMS's policy that a mistake in the execution of an arrangement (inadvertent or even intentional on the part of one party) may throw an arrangement out of compliance. The final rule made some clarifications on permissible profit shares for group practices, and made clarifications to the isolated transaction exception. It amended several exceptions to include as a requirement what used to be only safe harbor conditions for directed referral arrangements.

The final rule amended the definition of "indirect compensation arrangement," with the result that it is significantly more difficult to satisfy the definition, but that if the definition is satisfied, it will be more difficult for the arrangement to meet the exception for indirect compensation arrangements. It also revised the definition of "designated health service" to provide that a service provided by a hospital to an inpatient does not constitute a DHS payable, in whole or in part, by Medicare, if the furnishing of the service does not affect the amount of Medicare's payment to the hospital under the IPPS and other hospital prospective payment systems.[88]

It also made changes to the definition of "remuneration" to broaden the scope of CMS's interpretation of a statutory exclusion from the definition of remuneration.[89]

---

[88] *See* 85 Fed. Reg. at 77569-72.

[89] *See id.* at 77573-75.

2

Core Definitions, Terms Used in Exceptions, and "Special Rules"

OUTLINE

Understanding the core definitions, other defined terms and other terms of art is necessary to perform an assessment of any Stark issue, in order to determine whether the statute is implicated and, if it is, whether an exception (or waiver) is applicable and satisfied.

A. Core Definitions

Rather than proceeding alphabetically through the various definitions worth mentioning, this chapter first presents the definitions for the core terms that are necessary to be present for the Stark statute to be implicated. Recall that in order for the statute to be implicated there must be a "physician" who makes a "referral" of "designated health services" to an "entity" with which the physician or his or her "immediate family member" has a "financial relationship."[1] All of the words just quoted are terms of art, and thus the definitions for such terms (and others) are of crucial importance.

[1] 42 U.S.C. § 1395nn(a)(1). For ease of reference, the parenthetical "(or an immediate family member of such physician)" will be omitted. Future references to "physician" in connection with the Stark discussion often should be read to include the omitted parenthetical. An "immediate family member" or a "member of the physician's immediate family" is defined to include: husband or wife; birth or adoptive parent, child, or sibling; stepparent, stepchild, stepbrother or stepsister; father-in-law, mother-in-law, son-in-law, daughter-in-law, brother-in-law or sister-in-law; grandparent or grandchild; and spouse of a grandparent or grandchild. 42 C.F.R. § 411.351.

1. Physician (§ 411.351)/Immediate Family Member (§ 411.351)

The definition of "physician" is taken from the statute, and is mostly straightforward. A "physician" is a doctor of medicine or osteopathy legally authorized to practice medicine and surgery by the State in which s/he performs such function or action, and a doctor of dental surgery or of dental medicine who is legally authorized to practice dentistry by the State in which s/he performs such function and who is acting within the scope of his or her license. In addition, a doctor of podiatric medicine, a doctor of optometry, and a chiropractor may be a "physician" under certain circumstances.[2]

Importantly, for purposes of Stark, a physician and his or her professional corporation of which he or she is the sole owner are considered one and the same. Therefore, an arrangement between an entity or other party (such as a group practice) and such a professional corporation will be deemed to be an arrangement with the physician owner of the professional corporation.

An analysis of whether there is a financial relationship with an entity to which the physician refers DHS must consider more than just the individual physician. It should also consider whether there are any immediate family members who have a financial relationship with the entity to which the physician refers. In fact, physician employment agreements sometimes require the employed physician to disclose where their family members work. Consider the following example. Salesperson works for Lab and receives a commission on samples that are referred by physicians to Lab. Physician is the sister of Salesperson and refers samples to Lab, and because Physician works within Salesperson's assigned territory, Salesperson receives a commission on each of Physician's referred samples including the ones belonging to Medicare patients. Stark is therefore implicated. Physician is tagged with Salesperson's compensation arrangement and the terms of such arrangement. Because the Physician's deemed compensation arrangement impermissibly takes into account the volume or value of referrals for DHS, there is no exception that protects the arrangement.

---

[2] Section 1861(r) of the Social Security Act, 42 U.S.C. § 1395x(r).

2. Referral (§ 411.351)

"Referral" is defined as any request, order of, or the certifying or recertifying of the need for any DHS that is payable by Medicare;[3] however, personally performed services fall outside the definition.[4] "Personally performed" is to be taken literally—if a physician orders an X-ray for a Medicare patient, for example, and a technician performs the X-ray, this is a "referral" for the technical component (the taking of the X-ray) and not a personally performed service notwithstanding that the ordering physician may be the physician who supervises the X-ray. If the same physician interprets the X-ray, however, this is not a "referral" for the professional component (interpretation of the X-ray) because the physician personally performed the service.

CMS traditionally and justifiably has been skeptical of patients self-referring and thereby leaving a physician with no referral,[5] but there are circumstances in which there truly is a patient self-referral. For example, if a physician were to provide a patient with a complete list of nearby imaging facilities at which the patient could receive an X-ray, and such list is not weighted in any particular way (e.g., same size font, in alphabetical order or ranked by proximity), and the patient happens to choose the facility in which the physician has an ownership interest, there would not be a "referral" from the physician. Where such a *patient self-referral* has been made, the physician would do well to document how it was made.

A referral may be imputed to the referring physician if such physician directly or indirectly controls a referral made by another

---

[3] Strictly speaking, a "referral" means a referral for DHS, and thus the term "referral for DSH" is redundant. However, for clarity, sometimes the term "referral for DHS" is used herein. Likewise, "referral" may be used in its generic sense, i.e., the ordering of services irrespective of whether they are DHS.

[4] 42 C.F.R. § 411.351 (Referral).

[5] Consider the situation in which a patient drives himself or herself to a hospital emergency department. At that point there is a patient self-referral, but no services have been ordered. That patient may believe that she needs an X-ray, and she may truly need one, but the patient cannot self-order an X-ray. As soon as the employed hospitalist orders the X-ray there is a "referral" for DHS by a physician who has a financial relationship with the hospital-entity. Now suppose the hospitalist later "decides" the patient should be admitted for inpatient care. If the hospitalist does not have admitting privileges, and therefore can only recommend admission, some other physician would be charged for the referral/admission.

individual. For example, a mid-level associate such as a physician assistant or a nurse practitioner may order services according to their authorized scope of practice, but if they do so pursuant to a protocol or plan of care established by a physician, the physician may be charged with a referral for DHS or other business generated.

The following example illustrates the breadth of the definition of "referral." Suppose a Medicare patient presents to the emergency room at a hospital and is examined by a hospitalist who does not have admitting authority at the hospital. The hospitalist determines that the patient needs inpatient care, and makes the recommendation to admit the patient. A physician owner of the hospital signs off on the admitting order. The physician owner is charged with a "referral" (and not the hospitalist) for purposes of Stark, and the referral must satisfy an ownership exception.

By statute, a referral does not include a request by (1) a pathologist for clinical diagnostic laboratory tests and pathological examination services, (2) a radiologist for diagnostic radiology services, or (3) a radiation oncologist for radiation therapy or ancillary services necessary for and integral to the provision of radiation therapy, if, in each case, (1) the request results from a consultation initiated by another physician and (2) the tests or services are furnished by or under the supervision of the pathologist, radiologist, radiation oncologist, or under the supervision of the corresponding type of physician in the same group practice.[6]

Note that in order for DHS ordered by a pathologist, radiologist or radiation oncologist to not be considered a referral from such a physician, the DHS must be ordered pursuant a "consultation," which itself is a term of art, with specific requirements. For example, a "consultation" requires that the request and need for the consultation be documented in the patient's medical record, and that after the consultation is provided, the physician prepares a written report of his or her findings, which is provided to the physician who requested the consultation.[7]

---

[6] Note, however, that whereas pathologists typically do not order services, it is not unusual for a pathologist to order "special stains," and when they do so on behalf of a Medicare patient they make a "referral." Likewise, if a radiologist orders additional images for a Medicare patient, this too would be a "referral."

[7] *See* 42 C.F.R. § 411.351 (consultation).

If a pathologist or radiologist or radiation oncologist is not tagged with a referral for DHS because the DHS ordered was pursuant to a "consultation," does that mean that the physician who requested the consultation is instead tagged with a referral for the DHS that was ordered? Although the statutory language on this point is not drafted well,[8] the answer from CMS appears to be yes. However, because CMS has a very specific definition of "consultation," not every referral of a patient from a generalist to a specialist will mean that the requesting physician will be tagged with any DHS ordered by the consulting physician.

In the 1992 proposed rule on Stark I, CMS said:

> For purposes of Medicare coverage, a "consultation" is a professional service furnished to a patient by a physician (the consultant) at the request of the patient's attending physician. A consultation includes the history and examination of the patient as well as a written report that is transmitted to the attending physician for inclusion in the patient's permanent record. If, in the course of that consultation, the consulting physician deems it necessary to order clinical laboratory services, those services may not be ordered from a laboratory in which the referring physician has a financial interest. Therefore, when a physician refers a patient for a consultation, it would be prudent for the

---

[8] Section 1887(h) provides:

> (5) Referral; referring physician.—
>
> (A) Physicians' services.—Except as provided in subparagraph (C), in the case of an item or service for which payment may be made under part B, the request by a physician for the item or service, including the request by a physician for a consultation with another physician (and any test or procedure ordered by, or to be performed by (or under the supervision of) that other physician), constitutes a "referral" by a "referring physician".

The language "the request by a physician for a consultation with another physician (and any test or procedure ordered by, or to be performed by (or under the supervision of) that other physician) constitutes a 'referral' by a 'referring physician'" can be read as charging *the requesting physician* with a referral for any DHS ordered by the consulting physician. The language can also be read, however, as meaning that tests and procedures that are ordered by *the consulting physician* are referrals.

referring physician to provide to the consultant a list of laboratories from which the consulting physician should not order services.

Other referrals, such as sending a patient to a specialist who assumes responsibility for furnishing the appropriate treatment, or providing a list of referrals for a second opinion, are not "consultations" or "referrals" that would trigger the laboratory services use prohibition.[9]

According to the above, a referral of a patient is not the same as a referral of DHS, and where one physician refers a patient to a specialist who assumes responsibility for treatment of the patient, the first physician is not charged with any referrals of DHS made by the second physician—unless, of course, the two physicians have entered into a circumvention scheme. Although CMS's conception of what constitutes a referral for DHS evolved (most notably by reversing its initial view that a personally performed service is a "referral"), the view expressed by the 1992 proposed rule seems to have remained constant.

In the 1998 proposed rule for Stark II, CMS quoted from the above passage from the 1992 proposed rule. It then stated:

We would like to clarify that a consultation occurs whenever a physician requests that a patient see another physician, such as a particular specialist, but the original physician retains control over the care of the patient, including any care related to the condition that prompted the consultation. Section 1877(h)(5)(A) implies that a "consultation" is still a consultation even if the consultant physician takes the initiative to order, perform, or supervise the performance of, tests for the patient. The consultant physician, as we noted in the preamble of the August 1995 rule, must provide the original physician with a report. Nonetheless, we regard this as a consultation as long as it is the original physician who gathers information from

[9] 57 Fed. Reg. at 8795 (emphasis supplied).

> the consultant physician about his or her examination of the patient and any test results and then makes a decision about how to proceed with the patient's care.
>
> Conversely, the original physician has not arranged for a consultation, but instead has made a referral, in situations in which the specialist takes over the patient's care for purposes of the condition that prompted the referral [of the patient]. For example, a physician might send a patient to a specific cardiologist, who examines the patient thoroughly, sends a report to the attending physician but is the only one who sees the patient thereafter for the purpose of treating a heart problem.[10]

In other words, a report must be sent by the second physician to the first physician in order for there to be a consultation, but the fact that one is sent does not mean that there is necessarily a consultation; rather it depends on which physician remains responsible for the patient's care for the condition that prompted the referral of the patient.

In the Phase I final rule, CMS adopted the definition of "consultation" in section 411.351 that is unchanged as of today. Along the way, CMS stated:

> The final rule adopts a very broad interpretation of a consultation. We want to make clear that this definition is only for the very limited purpose of determining when a pathologist's, diagnostic radiologist's, or radiation oncologist's ordering of DHS from a facility with which he or she has an otherwise prohibited financial relationship will not prohibit submission of a claim to Medicare.[11]

Note that the language "with which he or she has an otherwise prohibited financial relationship" relates back to "a pathologist's,

[10] 63 Fed. Reg. at 1693.
[11] 66 Fed. Reg. at 873.

diagnostic radiologist's, or radiation oncologist's ordering of DHS." From this we see that CMS was concerned with a prohibited financial relationship between the *consulting* physician and a DHS entity. This indicates that CMS does not read the statutory language as tagging the requesting physician with DHS ordered by the consulting physician.[12,13]

But then CMS muddies the waters with these statements in the Phase I preamble:

> Finally, we want to make clear that section 1877(h)(5)(C) of the Act only protects the referral of DHS from the pathologist, diagnostic radiologist, or radiation oncologist to the DHS provider. If the DHS provider— (1) knows or has reason to suspect that the referral originated from the referring physician, and (2) has a direct or indirect financial relationship with the referring physician, the DHS provider cannot submit a claim to Medicare for the DHS unless the financial relationship fits into an exception. Moreover, the referring physician may not make the referral to the consultant if he or she knows or has reason to suspect that the consultant will order DHS from an entity with which the referring physician has a direct or indirect financial relationship to which no exception applies.

The sentence starting "If the DHS provider . . ." may mean to say that the requesting physician is necessarily charged with the DHS ordered by the consulting physician and that the DHS entity would be prohibited from billing for the DHS if it knows or has reason to know the identity of the requesting physician (and therefore ought to know that it has an unexcepted financial relationship with the requesting physician). Or, this sentence may mean to say that the requesting physician is charged with the referral only if the requesting physician in effect ordered the DHS. (What does CMS mean by "the referral *originated* from the referring physician"?) Note that a

---

[12] 66 Fed Reg. at 873.

[13] 66 Fed. Reg. at 874.

few pages earlier in the preamble, CMS spoke of one physician using another as an "intermediary" in the ordering of DHS.[14] The next sentence in the passage quoted above ("Moreover, the referring physician may not make the referral . . .") then says that the requesting physician is prohibited from sending the patient to the consultant in the first place if he or she knows or has reason to know that the request will result in DHS ordered from an entity with which the requesting physician has an unexcepted financial relationship. But again, is this latter sentence saying that the referring physician is prohibited as a matter of course in making the referral of the patient to the consultant (including a consulting pathologist radiologist or radiation oncologist who would not be charged with a referral of DHS due to the statutory/regulatory exception on what constitutes a referral of DHS) if the referring physician has an unexcepted financial relationship with the DHS entity that receives the referral? Or does this sentence merely address the situation where the referring physician is using the consulting physician as an intermediary?

In any event, the Phase I preamble does not pull away from the idea that if a physician refers a patient to another physician and the second physician takes over control for treating the patient for the condition for which the patient was referred, the physician referring the patient is not charged with referrals of DHS with respect to items and services ordered by the second physician. Again, the requirements of a "consultation," including the report sent to the requesting physician, must be satisfied in order for the physician referring the patient to be charged with DHS ordered by the consulting physician.

Subsequent Stark rules did not change the definition of consultation or expound upon the guidance in the Phase I final rule.

3. Entity (§ 411.351)

The term "entity" can encompass both entities and individuals. An entity is "a physician's sole practice or a practice of multiple physicians or any other person, sole proprietorship, public or private agency or trust, corporation, partnership, limited liability company, foundation, nonprofit corporation, or unincorporated association

---

[14] *See* 66 Fed. Reg. at 871, 872.

that furnishes DHS."[15] Hospitals, DME suppliers, freestanding imaging facilities, home health agencies, labs, and many more are entities.

Prior to the FY 2009 IPPS final rule, only individuals and entities that billed Medicare were considered to be furnishing DHS. In that rule, however, CMS revised the definition of entity to provide that an entity furnishes DHS if it performs services that are billed as DHS. The revised definition of entity was aimed at certain "under arrangement" arrangements. Medicare allows hospitals (and other providers of services) to furnish (and bill for) services that they provide directly or "under arrangement." For example, two hospitals in a small community may decide that it is not economically feasible for them to duplicate the range of services they offer. Hospital A may send its inpatients needing magnetic resonance imaging (MRI) to Hospital B, which performs the MRI and bills Hospital A for the MRI but does not bill a payor for the MRI. Such patients would remain patients of Hospital A and Hospital A would be said to be furnishing (and billing for) the MRI services "under arrangement." Now suppose that Physician owns a freestanding MRI center with which Hospital A has an exclusive contract. If Physician is treating a patient of Hospital A and orders an MRI, Physician knows that the patient will be sent to Physician's MRI facility due to the exclusive contract. Under the revised definition of "entity," because Physician's MRI center would be performing services that are billed as DHS (by Hospital), the MRI center would be considered an "entity," and Physician's order of the MRI would be considered to be a referral for the MRI. Because of Physician's ownership interest in the MRI center, the referral would need to be protected by an ownership or general exception, but as a practical matter, the only potential exception available would be the rural provider exception. The purpose of the revised definition was to prevent overutilization of services and to discourage situations in which hospitals believed they were effectively prevented from having their own technology for fear of losing referrals from physicians who invested in such technology.

Although the purpose of the change in definition was aimed at hospital–physician group arrangements, and primarily at arrangements for outpatient services such as cardiac catheterizations, the

---

[15] 42 C.F.R. § 411.351 (Entity).

revised definition is implicated in other types of arrangements, such as one in which a physician group has an exclusive arrangement to furnish lab services to another physician group.

Following the revision of the definition to include the situation where an entity furnishes DHS if it performs services that are billed as DHS, the question arose as to what it means to perform services that are billed as DHS. Some guidance was given in the preamble of the FY 2009 IPPS final rule, and in the following year CMS sought comments on whether it should issue further guidance on what constitutes performing services billed as DHS and if so, the nature or content of such guidance.[16] However, no further guidance has been issued.[17]

The definition of entity contains a few exceptions. Although a physician or physician practice that bills Medicare is generally considered to be an entity, it is not an entity when it bills Medicare in accordance with the payment limitation imposed by the anti-markup rule.[18] The anti-markup rule[19] provides that where the same physician or other supplier (including physician group) bills for the technical component (TC) and/or the professional component (PC) of a diagnostic test that was ordered by the physician or other supplier (or ordered by a party related to such physician or other supplier through common ownership or control) the payment to the billing physician group or other supplier is effectively limited to what the billing group or other supplier paid the party performing the TC and/or the PC, unless an exception applies.[20] The purpose of the anti-markup rule

---

[16] *See* 74 Fed. Reg. at 61932.

[17] CMS posted on its self-referral web page a response to the comment received. It stated that the comments it received did not convince it to provide additional guidance. It concluded that the guidance provided in the FY 2009 IPPS final rule is sufficient in most cases to identify when a provider or supplier has "performed the DHS." It noted that parties may seek further guidance through the advisory opinion process. *See* https://www.cms.gov/Medicare/Fraud-and-Abuse/PhysicianSelfReferral/Definition_of_Entity.

[18] 42 C.F.R. § 411.351 (Entity).

[19] 42 C.F.R. § 414.50.

[20] The anti-markup rule could be implicated with respect to the TC, or the PC, or both or neither. Where the rule is implicated as to both the TC and the PC, the payment limitation could apply to both the TC and the PC, or one or the other, or neither.

is to prevent overutilization that may occur when, for example, a urology group contracts with a pathologist to examine biopsies of prostate core samples and would pay the pathologist (and his/her histologist) less than what the group could bill Medicare. Therefore, where the anti-markup rule is implicated *and* the payment limitation applies,[21] the risk of overutilization is addressed and it is not necessary for Stark to be applicable.

The definition of entity also excepts managed care organizations (which typically do not bill Medicare fee for service (FFS)), unless they are billing Medicare FFS under a reassignment.[22]

4. Designated Health Services (§ 411.351)

This term of art is defined to include: (1) clinical laboratory services; (2) physical therapy, occupational therapy, and outpatient speech-language pathology services; (3) radiology and certain other imaging services; (4) radiation therapy services and supplies; (5) durable medical equipment and supplies; (6) parenteral and enteral nutrients, equipment, and supplies; (7) prosthetics, orthotics, and prosthetic devices and supplies; (8) home health services; (9) outpatient prescription drugs; and (10 and 11) inpatient and outpatient hospital services.[23]

Only the services included in the definition of DHS invoke Stark. For example, services paid under the ambulatory surgery center fee schedule or the skilled nursing facility prospective payment system are not DHS, and thus referrals for such services are outside the purview of Stark. One of the keys to a Stark analysis is determining whether the services that may be performed under an arrangement[24]

---

[21] The exception in section 411.351 states that it is applicable in situations in "which the anti-markup provision is applicable," CMS construes this language to mean that the anti-markup rule is both implicated and the payment limitation applies, which makes sense given that if the payment limitation does not apply, the risk of overutilization is not addressed. If the anti-markup rule is implicated and the payment limitation applies to only the TC or only the PC, the exception to the definition of entity would apply only to the TC or PC, as applicable.

[22] 42 C.F.R. § 411.351 (definition of "Entity").

[23] 42 C.F.R. § 411.351 (Designated health services).

[24] When structuring an arrangement, unless it is certain that no DHS will be furnished, it is much safer to assume that at least some DHS will be furnished at least some of the time.

are encompassed within the definition of DHS. If the service being reviewed is not included, a Stark issue probably does not exist.[25]

In the 2020 final rule, CMS addressed the situation in which a referral for hospital services comes after the initial admission and diagnosis has been made. Typically, such additional services do not increase the payment the hospital receives.[26] The 2020 final rule modified the definition of DHS by providing "[f]or services furnished to inpatients by a hospital, a service is not a designated health service payable, in whole or in part, by Medicare if the furnishing of the service does not increase the amount of Medicare's payment to the hospital under [certain] prospective payment systems."[27]

There is another way in which CMS could have reached the result of not prohibiting a referral for services that do not increase the amount of Medicare's payment to the hospital. The statute provides that "[a] physician may not make a referral to the entity for the furnishing of designated health services *for which payment otherwise may be made under this title*, and that an entity may not present a claim or cause a claim to be presented for such prohibited referral."[28] The language "for which payment otherwise may be made under [Medicare]" could be construed to mean that a referral is prohibited only if it results in payment or additional payment by Medicare. On the other hand, it may also be construed to mean only that the service must qualify for Medicare payment in the first place (e.g., the service is covered by Medicare and is reasonable and necessary). This statutory language was brought to CMS's attention in an effort to address situations such as physician ownership of intraoperative neurological monitoring, and radiation therapy that was provided

---

[25] It is important to note that a financial relationship between a referring physician and an entity that is created through the furnishing of services that are not DHS must still be compliant, lest the relationship create a Stark problem when services that *are* DHS are referred by such physician to the entity.

[26] However, in some cases the additional services may increase the costs to the hospital to the point that it receives an additional, "outlier" payment.

[27] The prospective payment systems (PPS) in question are: the acute care hospital inpatient PPS; inpatient rehabilitation facility PPS; inpatient psychiatric facility PPS; and long-term care hospital PPS. *See* 42 C.F.R. § 411.351. CMS specifically declined to extend the DHS carve-out to the hospital outpatient PPS.

[28] Section 1877(a)(1)(A) and (B) of the Social Security Act, 42 U.S.C. § 1395nn(a)(1)(A) and (B) (emphasis added).

in a non-hospital setting but must now be ordered by the treating physician and provided on an inpatient basis due to an admission unrelated to the need for radiation therapy. As discussed above, CMS chose not to go this route, and instead effected a carve-out from the definition of DHS. However, CMS did not address this statutory language in the 2020 final rule, so some practitioners may be comfortable in relying on it in situations that involve a prospective payment system (PPS) to which the carve-out does not apply (e.g., hospital outpatient PPS).

5. Financial Relationship (§ 411.354)/Definition of Remuneration (§ 411.351)

a. Remuneration

Before discussing the types of financial relationships, it is necessary to consider the concept of "remuneration" which is the undercurrent running through all financial relationships.

Remuneration is broadly defined as "any payment or other benefit made directly or indirectly, overtly or covertly, in cash or in kind."[29] Thus, for example, where one party is providing services to another party, and the services are of a type for which one normally expects payment, remuneration is exchanged even if the giver of the services is not in fact paid for them.

The statute contains a few exclusions from the definition, which have been interpreted and sometimes narrowed by the regulations. The statute has always contained an exclusion for items, devices, and supplies that are used to collect, transport, process, or store specimens for the entity furnishing the items, devices, or supplies or are used to order or communicate the results of tests or procedures for the entity.[30] However, the exclusion contained certain limitations. Until the effective date of the 2020 final rule, the regulatory version of the exclusion read: "The furnishing of items, devices, or supplies (*not including surgical items, devices, or supplies*) *that are used solely* to collect, transport, process, or store specimens for the entity furnishing the items, devices, or supplies *or are used solely* to order or communicate the results of tests or procedures for the entity." The 2020 final

[29] 42 C.F.R. § 411.351 (Remuneration).

[30] Section 1877(h)(1)(C)(ii) of the Social Security Act.

rule removed the parenthetical "(not including surgical items, devices, or supplies)" from the exclusion, reasoning that CMS was

> no longer convinced that the mere fact that an item, device, or supply is routinely used as part of a surgical procedure means that the item, device, or supply is not used solely for one of the six purposes listed at section 1877(h)(1)(C)(ii) of the Act. Rather, the relevant inquiry for purposes of the physician self-referral law is whether the item, device, or supply is used solely for one or more of the [six] statutory purposes, regardless of whether the device is also classified as a surgical device.[31]

The six statutory purposes are:

1. Collecting specimens for the entity furnishing the items, devices, or supplies
2. Transporting specimens for the entity furnishing the items, devices, or supplies
3. Processing specimens for the entity furnishing the items, devices, or supplies
4. Storing specimens for the entity furnishing the items, devices, or supplies
5. Ordering tests or procedures for the entity furnishing the items, devices, or supplies
6. Communicating the results of tests or procedures for the entity furnishing the items, devices, or supplies[32]

At the same time CMS retained the "used solely" language in the exclusion, but revised its interpretation to mean that it is not enough that an item, device, or supply *could be* used for a purpose *other than* one or more of the six permitted purposes in order to take the furnishing of the item, device, or supply out of the exclusion and render

[31] *See* 85 Fed. Reg. at 77574.

[32] *See* section 1877(h)(i)(C)(ii); 42 U.S.C. § 1395nn(h)(1)(C)(ii); 42 C.F.R. § 411.351 (Remuneration).

it remuneration; instead, if the item, device is (1) *in fact* used solely for one of the statutory six purposes, and (2) its primary purpose is for one of the statutory six purposes it will not be considered remuneration. CMS gave the example of sterile gloves and other multi-use items. These can be used, and in fact may be used, for one of the statutory six purposes but their primary purpose is not one of the permitted purposes and they are not excluded from the definition of "remuneration" even if a particular physician in fact uses the item or device. CMS also emphasized that, although it was not finalizing a monetary limit for the carve-out from the definition of remuneration, it believes that the items carved out must be low value and that items, devices, or supplies provided to a physician must have little or no independent value to the physician:

> In this context, it is important to note that both the statute and our regulations provide that the items, devices, or supplies provided must serve a purpose for the entity providing the items, devices, or supplies; for example, collecting specimens for the entity. We believe that the phrase "for the entity" underscores that the items, devices, or supplies must have little, if any, independent value for the physician.[33]

The other two statutory exclusions from the definition of "remuneration" are: (1) the forgiveness of amounts owed for inaccurate tests or procedures, mistakenly performed tests or procedures, or the correction of minor billing errors;[34] and, (2) a payment made by an insurer or a self-insured plan to a physician to satisfy a claim, submitted on a FFS basis, for the furnishing of health services by that physician to an individual who is covered by a policy with the insurer or by the self-insured plan, if certain requirements are met.[35]

[33] See *id.* at 77575.

[34] Section 1877(h)(1)(C)(i), 42 U.S.C. § 1395nn(h)(1)(C)(i).

[35] Section 1877(h)(1)(C)(iii), 42 U.S.C. § 1395nn(h)(1)(C)(iii).

b. *Types of Financial Relationships*

A financial relationship may be an ownership or investment interest or compensation arrangement, and may be direct or indirect. Thus, there are four types of financial relationships.[36]

i. Direct Ownership or Investment Interest in an Entity (411.354(b))

Both the statute and the regulations provide that an ownership or investment interest in the entity may be through equity, debt, or other means, and includes an interest in an entity that holds an ownership or investment interest in any entity that furnishes DHS. An important consideration is that "[a]n ownership or investment interest in a subsidiary company is neither an ownership or investment interest in the parent company, nor in any other subsidiary of the parent, unless the subsidiary company itself has an ownership or investment interest in the parent or such other subsidiaries."[37]

According to the regulations, an ownership or investment interest includes, but is not limited to, stock, stock options other than those described in 411.354(b)(3)(ii)[38], partnership shares, limited liability company memberships, as well as loans, bonds, or other financial instruments that are secured with an entity's property or revenue or a portion of that property or revenue.

The definition of ownership or investment interest has specific exclusions in addition to the aforementioned one for stock options.[39] For example, an interest arising from a retirement plan, stock options and convertible securities prior to exercise or conversion, an unsecured loan that is subordinated to a credit facility, an "under arrangements" contract, or a security interest in equipment sold by

---

[36] *See* 42 C.F.R. § 411.354(a).

[37] *See id.* at § 411.354(b)(2). Paragraph (b)(2) adds the caveat that an ownership or investment interest in a subsidiary company may be part of an indirect financial relationship.

[38] The aforementioned carve-out for stock options in section 411.354(b)(3)(ii) is broad: "Stock options and convertible securities received as compensation until the stock options are exercised or the convertible securities are converted to equity (before this time the stock options or convertible securities are compensation arrangements, and not an ownership or investment interest)."

[39] *See id.* at § 411.354(b)(3).

a physician to a hospital are not ownership and investment interests that create a direct financial relationship.[40]

The 2020 final rule added to the list of exclusions a titular ownership/investment interest that excludes the ability or right to receive the financial benefits of ownership or investment, including, but not limited to, the distribution of profits, dividends, proceeds of sale, or similar returns on investment.[41]

The fact that the statute states in broad terms that an ownership or investment interest in the entity *may* be through equity, debt, or other means, raises that question as to how much authority CMS has to sweep certain rights or relationships into an ownership or investment interest. On the one hand, the Secretary has broad authority under sections 1102(a) and 1871(a) of the Social Security Act, but on the other hand the words "ownership" and "investment interest" should be given their ordinary meanings, and broad rulemaking authority does not encompass arbitrary and capricious distinctions.

It should also be noted that, on its face, section 411.354(b)(3) does not purport to present a complete list of items or transactions that do not constitute an ownership/investment interest (such a list would be impossible to compile). Thus, the facts that CMS provides that neither an unsecured loan subordinated to a credit facility, nor a security interest held by a physician in equipment sold by the physician to a hospital and financed through a loan from the physician to the hospital, is an ownership/investment interest does not mean that other unsecured loans or other security interests are necessarily ownership/investment interests.

ii. Indirect Ownership or Investment Interest in an entity (411.354(b)(5))

An indirect ownership or investment interest exists if, between the referring physician and the entity furnishing DHS, there exists an unbroken chain of any number of persons or entities (but no less than one) having an ownership or investment interest between them.[42] The

[40] *Id.*

[41] 42 C.F.R. § 411.354(b)(3)(vi).

[42] *See id.* at § 411.354(b)(5)(i)(A).

entity furnishing DHS need not know the precise composition of the chain in order to create the indirect relationship.[43]

It is important to remember that regardless of whether a physician has a direct or only an indirect ownership or investment interest in a DHS entity, an ownership or service-based exception would be needed to protect his or her referrals for DHS to the entity. For example, it would not matter if a physician has an ownership interest in a home health agency (HHA) or in the parent of the HHA—the exceptions analysis would be the same.

iii. Direct Compensation Arrangement (411.354(c)(1))/ Physician Organization (411.351)

A direct compensation exists if remuneration passes directly between the referring physician and the "entity furnishing DHS without any intervening persons or entities."[44]

The stand-in-the-shoes (SITS) rule creates a direct compensation arrangement between certain physicians and an entity notwithstanding the lack of privity of contract between the physician and the entity. Specifically, a physician owner of his or her "physician organization" is considered to stand in the shoes of his or her physician organization and is deemed to have the same compensation arrangement that his or her physician organization has with the DHS entity and on the same terms.[45]

---

[43] *See id.* at § 411.354(b)(5)(ii).

[44] *See id.* at § 411.354(a)(2). A caveat is that the language "without any intervening person or entities" should not be taken too literally. The Phase I final rule contained a definition of "direct financial relationship" at 411.354(a)(2), which stated "[a] direct financial relationship exists if remuneration passes between the referring physician (or a member of his or her immediate family) and the entity furnishing DHS without any intervening persons or entities (not including an agent of the physician, the immediate family member, or the entity furnishing DHS)." *See* 66 Fed. Reg. at 958. The parenthetical beginning "not including" disappeared, without any proposal or explanation by the time the Phase II rule was published, but parenthetical or no, the interposition of an agent or bagman between the referring physician and the entity would likely be disregarded by the government and any court faced with the issue.

[45] As originally promulgated in the Phase III final rule, the SITS rule was much broader. Immediately after the publication of the Phase II final rule on September 5, 2007, CMS learned that the application of the SITS rule created unanticipated problems for academic medical centers and others, and on November 15, 2007, CMS issued

For example, where a physician group practice has an agreement with a hospital to provide emergency call services, each owner of the group practice will be deemed to have the same arrangement with the hospital as set forth in the agreement between the group practice and the hospital. If there is a problem with the agreement between the group practice and the hospital (e.g., the compensation under the agreement is not fair market value), each physician owner of the group practice will have a nonconforming compensation arrangement with the hospital and each owner physician's referrals for designated health services to the hospital during the period of noncompliance of the agreement will be tainted. Non-owner physicians in the group practice would not be tagged with that relationship. Instead, one would have to analyze whether the non-owner physicians would have an indirect compensation arrangement (discussed below) with the entity furnishing the DHS based on an unbroken chain of financial relationships that would run physician—group practice (compensation arrangement)—hospital (compensation arrangement), and, if so, whether that indirect compensation could meet an exception.

Note that only "true" owners of a physician organization are required to stand in the shoes of their physician organization. Nominal or titular physician owners, such as the physician owner holding title to stock in a friendly professional corporation in a state with a corporate practice of medicine prohibition, are not required to stand in the shoes of their physician organization. However, the parties may voluntarily elect to treat such an owner or other physician non-owner as standing in the shoes of the physician organization (which rarely would be advantageous). Note also, that a physician and his or her solely owned professional corporation are treated as one and the same. That is, even before the SITS principle was finalized, a physician and his or her solely owned professional corporation were considered one and the same,[46] so that a physician was deemed to

---

a final rule (without a previous comment period) delaying the effective date of the SITS rule for certain compensation arrangements. *See* 72 Fed. Reg. 64161. The present version of the SITS rule was promulgated in the FY 2009 IPPS final rule. *See* 73 Fed. Reg. at 48691-92, 48693-699.

[46] *See* 42 C.F.R. 411.351 (definition of "Physician").

have the same financial relationship with a DHS entity that his or her solely owned professional corporation had with that DHS entity.

It is important to remember that SITS only applies to physicians. CMS proposed, but did not finalize an analogous SITS principle for entities.[47] Accordingly, SITS is relevant only when considering the physician side of an arrangement.

Because SITS applies only to physician owners of a "physician organization," it is important to understand what that term means. It is defined as "a physician, a physician practice, or a group practice that complies with the requirements of § 411.352." In other words, it is a solo or multi-physician group whose primary purpose is to deliver professional physician services. The fact that an entity may include or consist entirely of physicians does not mean, by itself, that the entity is a "physician organization." CMS has published several FAQs that give examples of what are not physician organizations.[48]

iv. Indirect Compensation Arrangement (411.354(c)(2))

Traditionally, the indirect compensation arrangement analysis has been among the most, if not the most, complex analysis in all of Stark despite CMS's not infrequent efforts to make it less so.[49]

The 2020 final rule made significant changes to the "aggregate compensation" component of the definition of "indirect compensation arrangement," which has made the analysis even more complex.

Prior to the effective date of the 2020 final rule, an indirect compensation arrangement exists if: (1) there is an unbroken chain of any number of (but not less than one) financial relationships between the referring physician and the entity furnishing DHS; (2) the referring physician receives aggregate compensation from the person or entity with which the physician has a *direct* financial relationship that varies with or otherwise reflects the volume or value of referrals

---

47 *See* 73 Fed. Reg. at 48689, 48692-93, 48699-48700.

48 *See* https://www.cms.gov/Medicare/Fraud-and-Abuse/PhysicianSelfReferral/Downloads/FAQs-Physician-Self-Referral-Law.pdf.

49 Practitioners should keep in mind that if the referring physician in question is an owner of a group practice or other "physician organization" that has a compensation arrangement with a DHS entity, the referring physician will stand in the shoes of the physician organization and have a direct compensation arrangement with the DHS entity.

or other business generated by the referring physician, "regardless of whether the individual unit of compensation satisfies the special rules on unit-based compensation under paragraphs (d)(2) or (d)(3) of [section 411.354]";[50] and (3) the entity furnishing DHS has actual knowledge of, or acts in reckless disregard or deliberate ignorance of the fact that the referring physician receives aggregate compensation that varies with or otherwise reflects the value or volume of referrals or other business generated by the referring physician for the entity furnishing the DHS.[51]

In the 2020 final rule, CMS revised the "aggregate compensation" element of the indirect compensation arrangement analysis to make it more difficult for parties to have an indirect compensation arrangement. The new definition, as modified further in the CY 2022 Physician Fee Schedule (PFS) final rule,[52] struck the language "regardless

---

[50] 42 C.F.R. § 411.354(c)(2)(ii) (2019). Subparagraph (c)(2)(ii) then added

> If the financial relationship between the physician (or immediate family member) and the person or entity in the chain with which the referring physician (or immediate family member) has a direct financial relationship is an ownership or investment interest, the determination of whether the aggregate compensation varies with or otherwise reflects the volume or value of referrals or other business generated by the referring physician will be measured by the non-ownership or non-investment interest closest in the chain to the referring physician (or immediate family member).

The use of the definite article "the," as in "[I]f *the* financial relationship . . ." should not be read to mean that the rule in paragraph (c)(2)(ii) is necessarily the only aggregate compensation test that is applicable where there is a direct financial relationship based on an ownership or investment interest. The same physician who has a direct ownership or investment interest may also have a compensation arrangement that must be analyzed in accordance with the beginning language of paragraph (c)(2)(ii).

[51] *See id.* at § 411.354(c)(2). If the group practice or other entity with which referring physician has a direct financial relationship is related to the DHS entity by ownership or common control, CMS may take the position that the knowledge test in paragraph (c)(2)(iii) is necessarily met. In any event, when structuring an arrangement to avoid meeting the definition of an "indirect compensation arrangement," it can be risky business to rely solely on the absence of knowledge that the aggregate compensation test is satisfied. Some DHS entities will require in their agreements with group practices or other entities that employ or contract with physicians a representation and warranty that the aggregate compensation test is not met.

[52] The preamble to the CY 2022 PFS has a detailed discussion of the definition of "indirect compensation arrangement." *See* 86 Fed. Reg. at 65344-53.

of whether the individual unit of compensation satisfies the special rules on unit-based compensation . . ." from the aggregate compensation test, and adds language that requires that the amount of compensation that the physician (or immediate family member) receives *per individual unit* compensation that has at least one of the following features in order for the test to be satisfied:

1. It is not fair market value for items or services actually provided.
2. It could increase as the number or value of the physician's referrals to the entity furnishing DHS increases, or could decrease as the number or value of the physician's referrals to the entity decreases.
3. It could increase as the amount or value of the other business generated by the physician for the entity furnishing DHS increases, or could decrease as the amount or value of the other business generated by the physician for the entity furnishing DHS decreases.
4. It is payment for the lease of office space or equipment or for the use of premises or equipment.[53]

By striking the language "regardless of whether individual unit of compensation satisfies the special rules on unit-based compensation," the revised definition of indirect compensation provides that non-tiered unit-based or percentage compensation arrangements will not meet the definition (provided that the new individual unit compensation test is not met).

---

[53] Romanette (iv) was added by the CY 2022 PFS final rule. Following the 2020 final rule, CMS realized that the revised definition had the unintended consequence of allowing per click leasing arrangements to escape scrutiny. Under the pre-2020 final rule version of the indirect compensation analysis, a per click leasing arrangement would fail the exception for indirect compensation arrangements, but under the 2020 final rule version of the aggregate compensation test, provided that individual unit of compensation to the referring physician was fair market value and could not increase/decrease as the number or value of the physician's referrals to the entity furnishing DHS or other business generated increased/decreased, there would not be an indirect compensation arrangement and therefore the exception would not be reached and the per click lease would escape scrutiny. Therefore, in the CY 2022 PFS final rule CMS baked into the formula for the aggregate compensation test per click lease arrangements in which the per click fee inures to the benefit of the referring physician.

Example: Physician-owned lithotripsy company (Company) enters into an under arrangements agreement (Agreement) with Hospital under which Hospital pays Company $X for each lithotripsy procedure performed on behalf of Hospital (and not $X+ or $X- depending on how many procedures are performed). Physician is an owner of Company and also refers DHS to Hospital. Because Company is not a "physician organization," Physician will not have a direct compensation arrangement with Hospital based on Agreement, and at most would have an "indirect compensation arrangement" with Hospital based on Agreement. Because the financial relationship that Physician has with the entity with which she has a direct financial relationship (Company) is an ownership/investment interest, the compensation arrangement closest to Physician (here, Agreement) is used to determine whether the aggregate compensation varies with the volume or value of referrals or other business generated by Physician to Hospital and whether the amount of compensation Physician receives per individual unit meets the conditions in section 411.354(c)(2)(ii)(A)(2). Physician may or may not have an indirect compensation arrangement with Hospital based on Agreement (there are not enough facts here to make that determination), but Physician will not have such an indirect compensation arrangement based on the even (non-tiered) payment formula of $X for each procedure. Prior to the 2020 final rule, that payment formula may have (depending on other facts) resulted in an indirect compensation arrangement between Physician and Hospital.

Increasing the complexity of the indirect compensation arrangement analysis even further, CMS added a rule for determining whether the individual unit compensation is measured by item, service, or time.[54]

[54] 42 C.F.R. § 411.354(c)(2)(ii)(B). The preamble to the CY 2022 PFS final rule contains an extended discussion of how unit compensation is to be determined. *See* 86 Fed. Reg. at 65347-48, 65351-53.

B. Definitions and Terms of Art for Requirements in Various Exceptions

1. Set in Advance/Amending Compensation Terms

a. Set in Advance

Several of the compensation exceptions, typically those that call for a written agreement, require that the compensation paid under the arrangement be "set in advance." According to CMS, the "'set in advance' requirement is an important safeguard to prevent parties from adjusting, including retrospectively adjusting, the compensation under an arrangement in a manner that takes into account the volume or value of a physician's referrals."[55] A fixed amount per period (e.g., month or year) would be set in advance, but CMS has also taken a formulaic approach to set in advance. Thus, per hourly compensation where the per hour amount is fixed would qualify as set in advance. Per unit ("per click") and percentage compensation also qualify as set in advance.[56] For the exception for value-based arrangements with meaningful downside financial risk to the physician and for the exception for value-based arrangements promulgated in the 2020 final rule, CMS provided that only the *methodology* for determining compensation must be set in advance.[57]

There is a deeming rule at section 411.354(d)(1) for set in advance. CMS describes it as "merely a deeming provision and parties are free to confirm satisfaction of the requirement another way,"[58] but it is difficult to imagine how one could satisfy the set in advance requirements if the provisions in the deeming rule are not met. The deeming rule states that compensation is deemed to be set in advance if the aggregate compensation, a time-based or per-unit-of-service–based amount, or a specific formula for calculating the compensation is set out in writing before the furnishing of the items or services (including office space and equipment) for which the compensation is to be paid. The compensation formula must be set forth in sufficient

---

55 *See* 85 Fed. Reg. at 77579.

56 Percentage compensation originally was not considered set in advance, but CMS reversed its position in the Phase II final rule.

57 *See* 85 Fed. Reg. at 77518.

58 *See id.* at 77515.

detail so that it can be objectively verified.[59] The deeming rule then provides that compensation that is modified after the inception of the arrangement may qualify as set in advance if, prior to the furnishing of the items, services, office space, or equipment for which the modified compensation is to be paid, the formula for determining it is set forth in writing in sufficient detail so that it can be objectively verified.[60] It also adds that the special rule allowing a 90-day grace period for obtaining a writing (section 411.354(e)(4)) cannot be used to get around the afore-mentioned requirements for modified compensation to be deemed set in advance.[61]

b. Amending Compensation Terms

In the FY 2009 IPPS final rule, CMS reversed the position it took in the Phase III final rule and stated in preamble language that the compensation terms or rental charges may be amended during the term of an agreement.[62] CMS conditioned the ability of parties to make mid-term amendments (including during the first year of the agreement) on: (1) the arrangement still satisfying an applicable exception, (2) the amended compensation or rent being determined before the amendment goes into effect, (3) the formula for the amended compensation or rent not taking into account the volume or value of referrals or other business generated, and (4) the amended compensation or rent terms remaining in place for at least one year from the date of the amendment.[63] This procedure applies to arrangements that are

---

[59] 42 C.F.R. § 411.354(d)(1)(i).

[60] 42 C.F.R. § 411.354(d)(1)(ii)(C).

[61] *Id.* ("Paragraph (e)(4) of this section does not apply for purposes of this paragraph (d)(1)(ii)(C)").

[62] 73 Fed. Reg. at 48697.

[63] *Id.* As a practical matter, the FY 2009 IPPS final rule required only that any particular amended compensation be *scheduled* to remain in effect for a year, and did not require it to actually last for a year. This circumstance can arise because the parties may amend the compensation terms of an agreement mid-term and then, before a year has passed, amend the terms again. In the Explanatory Guidance for the COVID blanket waivers, CMS said that it "has historically interpreted and continues to interpret preamble guidance in the [FY 2009 IPPS final rule] to allow a second or subsequent amendment of the remuneration terms of a compensation arrangement, even within the first year after an initial amendment. . . ." *See* https://www.cms.gov/files/document/explanatory-guidance-march-30-2020-blanket-waivers-section-1877g-social-security-act.pdf.

structured to meet an exception that requires a one-year term, such as the exception for personal services arrangements and the exceptions for space and equipment rentals. The fair market value exception does not fall into this category.

In the 2020 final rule, CMS amended section 411.354(d)(1) to add a new subparagraph (ii), which provides that the compensation terms may be amended at any time during the arrangement, without need to extend the term of the agreement, provided certain requirements are met.[64] CMS made clear that the paragraph (ii) of section 411.354(d)(1) is not a deeming rule—if parties wish to amend compensation terms during an arrangement they must abide by the requirements of this subparagraph.[65]

2. Fair Market Value

Fair market value has a specific and unique definition for purposes of Stark. The 2020 final rule simplified somewhat the definition of fair market value, and removed from the previous definition a reference to the volume or value of referrals. The 2020 revised definition of fair market value has three parts. First, there is a "general" definition of "fair market value," which is the value in an arm's-length transaction, consistent with the "general market value" of the subject transaction. "General market value" is in turn defined as the price that would result from arms-length bargaining value between well-informed parties that are not in a position to generate business for each other. Second, there is a specialized definition for the rental of equipment, which is the value in an arm's-length transaction of rental property for general commercial purposes (not taking into account its intended use), consistent with the general market value of the subject transaction. Third, there is a specialized definition for the rental of office space, namely, the value in an arm's-length transaction of rental property for general commercial purposes (not taking into account its intended use), without adjustment to reflect the additional value the prospective lessee or lessor would attribute to the proximity or convenience to the lessor where the lessor is a potential source of

---

64 *See* 85 Fed. Reg. at 77591, 77594.

65 *See id.* at 77594.

patient referrals to the lessee, and consistent with the general market value of the subject transaction.[66]

When assessing the fair market value component of a proposed arrangement, it can often be beneficial to engage an independent health care valuator who has experience working with the unique aspects of the requirements of Stark.

It is important to remember that valuing a proposed arrangement is outside the scope of an attorney's duties and obligations. A qualified valuation professional should be identified and tasked with conducting a valuation analysis.

Note that all but one of the compensation exceptions that have a fair market value requirement require that compensation be "fair market value," or "consistent with fair market value." For those exceptions, CMS's policy is that the compensation must not be greater or less than the range of fair market value. CMS has been urged to define "consistent with fair market value" to mean at least fair market value when the physician or immediate family member is paying compensation under an arrangement with an entity, and no more than fair market value when the physician or immediate family member is receiving compensation under the arrangement. Such a definition would not cause any fraud or abuse concerns, and would alleviate concerns that an arrangement could be found to be out of compliance. However, CMS has declined to adopt such a definition. The personal service arrangements (PSA) exception, which is statutory, sensibly provides that compensation to a physician (or his or her immediate family member or to a group practice) cannot *exceed* fair market value.[67]

3. Compensation That Takes into Account the Volume or Value of Referrals or Other Business Generated

The 2020 final rule added definitions for compensation to or from a physician that takes into account the volume or value of referrals or other business generated. Compensation from an entity to a physician

---

[66] 42 C.F.R. § 411.351 (Fair market value).

[67] Section 1877(e)(3)(A)(v), 42 U.S.C. § 1395nn(e)(3)(A)(v); 42 C.F.R. § 411.357(d)(1)(v).

takes into account the volume or value of referrals (or other business generated) if the formula used to calculate the compensation includes the physician's referrals to the entity (or other business generated by the physician for the entity) as a variable, resulting in an increase or decrease in the compensation that positively correlates with the number or value of the physician's referrals to the entity.[68] The 2020 final rule stressed that the question of whether compensation takes into account the volume or value of referrals/other business generated is answered solely by the formula itself, thus causing the demise of CMS's former view that fixed compensation can take into account the volume or value of referrals/other business generated if it exceeds fair market value.[69]

The positive correlation ("if X then Y") model that CMS adopted for purposes of determining when compensation to a physician (or immediate family member) takes into account the volume or value of referrals or other business generated is an awkward fit (or perhaps fits too well) for those exceptions that allow an indirect taking into account. For example, a "group practice" (which status is necessary for the physician services exception and practically necessary for the in-office ancillary services exception) is permitted to pay "physicians in the group practice" a profit share or a productivity bonus that only indirectly takes into account the volume or value of referrals,[70] and the electronic health records (EHR) and cybersecurity exceptions also permit an indirect taking into account.[71] The new definition of "takes into account" does not distinguish between directly and indirectly

---

68 42 C.F.R. § 411.354(d)(5)(i) and (ii). The final rule also added definitions for compensation from a physician to an entity that takes into account the volume or value of referrals or other business. These definitions are the same as the ones for compensation from an entity to a physician, except that the words "negatively correlates" are used instead of "positively correlates." *See* 42 C.F.R. § 411.354(d)(6)(i) and (ii).

69 *See* 85 Fed. Reg. at 77538 ("If the methodology used to determine the physician's compensation or the payment from the physician does not fall squarely within the defined circumstances, the compensation is not considered to take into account the volume or value of the physician's referrals or other business generated by the physician, as appropriate, for purposes of the physician self-referral law").

70 There is no prohibition on a group practice from paying its physicians in a manner that directly or indirectly takes into account other business generated. *See* 42 C.F.R. § 411.352(i).

71 *See* 42 C.F.R. §§ 411.357(w)(6), (bb)(1)(i).

taking into account the volume or value of referrals/other business generated, and the "positive correlation" test would appear to sweep in indirect takings into account (but if that is not true it would mean that traditional structures that were well-accepted as indirect takings into account are now outside the taking into account prohibition altogether.) The group practice definition contains certain safe harbors for profit shares and productivity bonus methodologies, and the questions arise as to whether those are now the only safe methodologies and whether even the safe harbors are in conflict with the new definition of "takes into account." In that regard, CMS noted in the 2020 final rule that it requested comments on the deeming provisions in the group practice definition and in the exception for donations of EHR items and services as to what will be considered an indirect taking into account, and based on the comments received, it either believed it was unnecessary to provide guidance or was unable to do so.[72]

The upshot is that parties, particularly group practices, are left in doubt as to whether a particular compensation methodology only indirectly takes into account the volume or value of referrals (or other business generated, as applicable). Methods that have been traditionally used and are no more or less indirect than what are contained in the deeming rules (such as distributing DHS based on relative number of patient encounters) may continue to be accepted as indirect, or it may be that only the examples contained in the deeming rules will be considered indirect. Even the deemed methodologies are somewhat in doubt as they are arguably in conflict with the positive correlation test.

There is another problem with the positive correlation test. Presumably, CMS takes the view that a compensation arrangement under which a physician receives a productivity bonus of 15 percent of the DHS collected by the entity for his referrals would be a direct taking into account the volume or value of referrals or other business generated, and a court would likely agree. Yet, strictly speaking, there is not a direct correlation between the physician's referrals and the amount of his productivity bonus, for the simple reason that payors may not pay always (and maybe never pay) for the service. As a *practical* matter, under the compensation arrangement, the more the

---

[72] *See* 85 Fed. Reg. at 77539 (first column).

physician refers the greater his productivity bonus, but as a matter of mathematics, it is not true that every time the physician refers DHS or other business generated his compensation will increase. Take the example of an independent contractor physician who refers only a certain type of imaging that is considered experimental by certain payors. Some of the referrals will result in payment and some not. As another example, suppose an employed or contracted physician refers DHS that are sometimes paid and sometimes denied as not reasonable and necessary. Strictly speaking, it cannot be said that the more DHS such physician refers the more she will be paid.

Prior to the 2020 final rule, there was no definition of what takes into account the volume or value of referrals or other business, per se, but there was guidance on what does *not* take into account the volume or value of referrals or other business generated. According to the preamble of Phase I, "[a] compensation arrangement does not take into account the volume or value of referrals or other business generated between the parties if the compensation is fixed in advance and will result in fair market value compensation, and the compensation does not vary over the term of the arrangement in any manner that takes into account referrals or other business generated."[73]

There are several things worth noting about the Phase I commentary. First, it sets forth CMS's only real guidance on the volume or value of referrals/other business generated prior to the 2020 final rule and will be wholly or partially applicable to arrangements that began prior to the effective date of the 2020 final rule (January 19, 2021). Second, because the preamble language states what does not take into account the volume or value of referrals/other business generated it is akin to a safe harbor, so if not all of the conditions are met, one is free to argue that the arrangement did not take into account referrals or other business generated.[74] Third, the Phase I preamble

[73] *See* 66 Fed. Reg. at 877-78.

[74] However, as a practical matter a contested failure to meet all of the conditions of the safe harbor would likely result in a finding that the arrangement did take into account the volume or value of referrals/other business generated or that the failed condition is an independent ground for not meeting the exception at issue. For example, several of the exceptions that have some prohibition on the taking into account the volume or value of referrals also require that the compensation be set in advance and/or be consistent with, or not exceed, fair market value.

language was codified in the safe harbors for per-unit (per-click) compensation, but there is no safe harbor in the text of the regulations for percentage compensation. At the time the Phase I preamble language was issued, percentage compensation was not considered "set in advance" (one of the required elements of the safe harbor), but since the effective date of the Phase II final rule percentage compensation is considered set in advance. In the Phase III final rule, CMS stated it declined (without explanation) to modify the safe harbors to include percentage compensation, but there does not appear to be a principled basis for not doing so. In any event, safe harbor protection or no, if a percentage-based arrangement meets all of the conditions set forth in the Phase I preamble language, the Government would be hard pressed to say (at least with the period prior to the 2020 final rule's effective date) that the compensation arrangement takes into account the volume or value of referrals or other business generated.

a. Incident to

"Incident to" services are a particular component of the volume or value analysis. CMS's pronouncements on productivity bonuses and (the lack of) profit shares for services billed incident are not entirely clear.

In the Phase II final rule, speaking about the exception for *bona fide* employment arrangements, CMS stated:

> [T]he statute contemplates that employed physicians can be paid in a manner that directly correlates to their own personal labor, including labor in the provision of DHS. What the statute does not permit are payments for an employee's productivity in generating referrals of DHS performed by others (66 FR 876). Except as permitted under the group practice definition for employees of group practices, "incident to" DHS may not be the basis for productivity bonuses paid to employed physicians.[75]

[75] *See* 69 Fed. Reg. at 16085.

Thus stated, the preamble indicates that the employment exception prohibits only a productivity bonus based on incident to *DHS*. The context of the preamble discussion was the distinction between a personally performed DHS, which, in Phase I, CMS decided is not a referral, and a DHS that is entirely or partially performed by others, including incident to DHS. The preamble language does not say that physicians cannot be paid a productivity bonus based on incident to services that are not DHS—to the contrary, it indicates they can.[76] Because the prohibition in the employee exception is only on the direct or indirect taking into account the volume or value of referrals for DHS—and not on "other business generated"—the employment exception should be properly read as allowing productivity bonuses based on other business generated.[77] However, other discussions of productivity bonuses for employed physicians in the Phase II and Phase II final rules do not make a clear distinction between incident to DHS and incident to non-DHS (other business generated). For example, a chart on physician compensation under various exceptions that appears in the Phase II final rule shows that, under the

---

[76] Consider also the following excerpt from elsewhere in the Phase II final rule:

> Thus, all physicians, whether group practice physicians, employed physicians, or independent contractor physicians, can be compensated for personally performed DHS, whether self-referred or referred by someone else. (We note that, under the statute, productivity bonuses for services "incident to" personally performed services are only permitted for physicians in group practices.)

69 *See* Fed. Reg. at 16092. Here too, the discussion appears to be in the context of DHS. Thus, the statement that "productivity bonuses for services 'incident to' personally performed services are only permitted for physicians in group practices" should be read to mean "productivity bonuses for DHS services 'incident to' personally performed services are permitted only for physicians in group practices."

[77] In the 1998 proposed rule CMS stated:

> We would like to point out that because we have interpreted the concept of a "referral" to involve only a physician's requests for designated health services covered under Medicare or Medicaid, the new [proposed] requirement [to prohibit productivity bonuses under the employment exception for personally performed DHS] will in no way affect a physician's ability to receive a productivity bonus for any non-designated health services or noncovered services he or she refers or performs, or designated health services referred by another physician.

See 63 Fed. Reg. at 1701.

employment exception, physicians may be paid a productivity bonus on personally performed services without distinguishing between DHS and non-DHS.[78]

Although there are restrictions on paying a productivity bonus on incident to DHS, depending on which exception is considered, entities can pay physicians for supervising incident to services (regardless of whether such incident to services are DHS). However, the compensation for supervision must not throw the entire compensation arrangement out of fair market value if the exception has a fair market value requirement. In the Phase II final rule, CMS sounded a warning against overpaying physicians for supervising incident to services:

> Productivity bonuses based on supervising DHS raise a different issue. We are concerned that, in some cases, a payment for supervision services may merely be a proxy payment for having generated the DHS being supervised. In many cases, especially in hospitals, the supervision required under Medicare rules is minimal, and the supervisor need do nothing more than be present in the facility while conducting other work. Accordingly, we are concerned that such payments could mask improper cross-referral or circumvention schemes. We note that any payment for supervision services must meet the fair market value standard in the exception.[79]

Although the above passage seems to suggest that, at least in certain circumstances, supervision is minimal and therefore compensation for supervision should also be minimal, note that, under the Physician Fee Schedule (PFS), Medicare typically pays 100% of the approved amount for a supervised, incident to service performed by a non-physician practitioner (NPP), whereas Medicare will pay only 85% of the approved amount if the same service is performed by the NPP and billed under the NPP's number as an NPP service (and not as an incident to service). This suggests that the supervision of the

[78] *See* 69 Fed. Reg. at 16067.
[79] *See* 69 Fed. Reg. at 16087-88.

service is worth at least 15% of the PFS payment. In addition to the fact that the physician must make himself or herself available to do the supervision, the physician may incur more malpractice risk in a supervised, incident to service than in a service that is performed by an NPP without supervision. In any event, practitioners are strongly urged to have a competent fair market value expert appraise the worth of the physician's supervision in any arrangement in which the physician would be paid for supervising incident to services.

4. Commercially Reasonable

The 2020 final rule added a definition of commercially reasonable (prior to that rule CMS provided some guidance but no definition). The definition states that an arrangement is commercially reasonable if the arrangement furthers a legitimate business purpose of the parties to the arrangement and is sensible, considering the characteristics of the parties, including their size, type, scope, and specialty. Importantly, CMS added that an arrangement may be commercially reasonable even if it does not result in profit for one or more of the parties. Certain providers, including not-for-profit hospitals may, in order to fulfill their mission, need to hire physicians of a certain specialty in order to provide needed services, knowing that the payor mix and/or the low volume of needed services will result in a loss for the provider. On the other hand, an arrangement in which a hospital hires physicians of a certain specialty that results in a loss to the hospital but results in profits for the hospital for the outpatient and inpatient procedures performed by the physicians may draw considerable scrutiny both for purposes of Stark and the Anti-Kickback Statute. Some arrangements may present an obvious high risk such as where a physician rents office space to a hospital at a fair market value per square foot, but the amount of square foot space rented is much more than the hospital needs or likely will need in the future.

Note that the exceptions that require an arrangement to be commercially reasonable require the arrangement be so *in the absence of referrals for DHS*. For example, the lease exceptions use the language "commercially reasonable even if no referrals were made between the parties,"[80] and the employment exception requires the arrangement

---

[80] 42 C.F.R. §§ 411.357 (a)(6), (b)(5).

"be commercially reasonable even if no referrals were made to the employer."[81] In the 2020 final rule CMS made clear that the "in the absence of referrals" language in its various forms is part and parcel of the commercial reasonable analysis even though it is not in the definition of "commercially reasonable" itself.[82]

Note that in the 2020 final rule CMS added the language "[t]he arrangement would be commercially reasonable even if no referrals were made between the parties" to the fair market value compensation exception, which it was able to do because it is a regulatory exception. However, the PSA exception, which is a statutory exception, continues to read: "The aggregate services covered by the arrangement do not exceed those that are reasonable and necessary for the legitimate business purposes of the arrangement(s)." Depending on the exception needed to protect the arrangement, the presence or absence of the "in the absence of referrals" language can make a difference between meeting or not meeting the exception.

For example, suppose a physician prefers to send his or her samples to a particular lab. The physician requests that the lab place a phlebotomist in the physician's office to make it more convenient for patients to get blood draws and the lab is agreeable to leasing an appropriate amount of space at fair market value from the physician. The physician will send commercial pay patients to the lab, but without DHS referrals

---

[81] 42 C.F.R. § 411.357(c)(3).

[82] CMS said:

> In the proposed rule, we explained that we were not proposing to include the phrase "even if no referrals were made" in the definition of "commercially reasonable" because this qualifying phrase (or similar language) appears in the regulation text of many exceptions that require an arrangement to be commercially reasonable (84 FR 55791). Thus, it would be redundant to include the language in the definition of "commercially reasonable" itself. We were clear that we were not proposing to remove this qualifying language from the exceptions in which it appears. We believe that this qualifying language provides critical protection against program or patient abuse, as an arrangement must be commercially reasonable even if no referrals were made by the physician. . . . An arrangement whose purpose is to attract a physician's business, even if the parties claim this purpose, would not be commercially reasonable in the absence of the physician's referrals and, thus, would not satisfy this important requirement of the exceptions generally applicable to compensation arrangements that call for items or services to be provided by a physician.

See 85 Fed. Reg. at 77533-34.

from the lab, the lab's rental payments will exceed the revenue realized by the physician's referrals. In this example, because the potential exceptions are the space exception and the fair market value compensation exception, the arrangement would appear to fail the commercial reasonableness test. But consider this example. Suppose an orthopedic practice, which sees mostly Medicare patients, wishes to contract with a physician to read studies. The practice would pay the physician a per-read fee. The physician requires that the practice have a sufficient number of studies to make it worth her while to contract with the practice. If the arrangement were for less than a year term, it arguably would not meet the commercial reasonableness requirement of the fair market value exception, but if it were for at least a year, the arrangement could be protected under the PSA exception (assuming that the other requirements of the PSA exception were met).

When in doubt, the practitioner should consider engaging a competent valuation expert that provides opinions on commercial reasonableness. At the very least, the expert's opinion may provide an effective defense against a claim of a knowing Stark violation.

5. Directed Referral Requirement

In the Phase I final rule, CMS created a safe harbor through which compensation paid to an employed or contracted physician who is required to make referrals to a particular entity will not be considered to take into account the volume or value of referrals or other business generated. The safe harbor, as originally promulgated, provided that the directed referral requirement be set forth in a written agreement signed by the parties, and that the requirement contain exceptions for where (1) the patient expresses a preference for a different provider, practitioner, or supplier; (2) the patient's insurer determines the provider, practitioner, or supplier; or (3) the referral is not in the patient's best medical interests in the physician's judgment.[83]

---

[83] *See* 66 Fed. Reg. at 877, 959. The Phase II final rule added romanette (v) to section 411.354(d)(4), which provides that: (1) the required referrals relate solely to the physician's services covered by the scope of the employment or the contract and the directed referral requirement is reasonably necessary to effectuate the legitimate business purposes of the compensation relationship, and (2) that in no event may the physician be required to make referrals that relate to services that are not provided by the physician under the scope of his or her employment or contract.

In the 2020 final rule CMS amended several exceptions to provide that, where a DHS entity has a directed referral arrangement with a physician the hitherto safe harbor requirements, together with new section 411.354(d)(4)(vi), are now required as a condition of meeting the exception.[84] Romanette vi to section 411.354(d)(4) provides that neither the existence of the compensation arrangement nor the amount of the compensation may be contingent on the number or the value of the physician's referrals to a particular provider, practitioner, or supplier; however, it also provides that it is permissible for a directed referral arrangement to require the physician to refer a certain percentage of his or her referrals to a particular provider, practitioner, or supplier. Thus, a requirement that a physician refer 500 X-rays to the employer or refer $500,000 worth of DHS to the employer would not pass muster under new section 411.354(d)(4)(vi), but a requirement that the physician refer 100 percent of his or her DHS to the employer would be permissible. The rationale for the distinction seems to be that the former may encourage overutilization but the latter would not.[85]

6. Holdover Period

Prior to the CY 2016 PFS final rule, the holdover protection was for a maximum of six months, but, effective for new arrangements or arrangements that were in effect (including in a valid holdover period of not more than six months) as of January 1, 2016, holdover protection exists for an unlimited amount of time.[86] However, as CMS cautioned, parties need to be vigilant that the arrangement remains fair market value during the months or even years that the holdover is in effect.[87]

---

[84] The amended exceptions are: §§ 411.355(e), and 411.357(c), (d)(1), (d)(2), (h), (l), (p), and (z).

[85] The rationale holds up generally, but consider the situation in which a physician has a productivity bonus that is payable if she refers 35 percent of her DHS to her employer's related imaging facility, and discovers, near the end of the year that she is missing the target by a few percentage points and needs to order some more imaging services to come up to 35 percent.

[86] *See* 80 Fed. Reg. at 71321.

[87] *See id.* at 71319-20.

7. Rural Area

A rural area is an area that does not constitute an urban area.[88] An urban area is a Metropolitan Statistical Area (MSA) or New England County Metropolitan Area (NECMA), as defined by the Executive Office of Management and Budget (OMB);[89] or certain specified counties in New England.[90] For purposes of the rural provider exception, it is crucial to know whether the provider (or supplier) is located in a rural area as well as the extent to which the provider's or supplier's patients are in a rural area. Areas can switch from rural to urban or vice versa so it is necessary to use the latest information from CMS or OMB.

C. Special Rules

1. Special Rules on Compensation

Section 411.354(d)(2) and (d)(3) provide that unit-based compensation does not take into account the volume or value of referrals or other business generated if the compensation is set in advance, fair market value, and does not vary over the course of the arrangement in a manner that takes into account the volume or value of referrals or other business generated. As explained below, these rules have largely been nullified by the 2020 final rule.

The rules were introduced in the Phase I final rule, and codified the Phase I preamble guidance on what does not take into account the volume or value of referrals. The rules acted to protect non-tiered compensation arrangements. Thus, if an entity paid a physician, who refers imaging services $X for each read the physician performed, regardless of the number of reads, the compensation arrangement would be deemed not to take into account the volume or value of referrals or other business generated (provided the other requirements of (d)(2) and (d)(3) were met). However, if, instead, the hospital paid $X for each read up to the first 50 reads, and $X+ for each

[88] 42 C.F.R. § 411.351 (Rural area).

[89] The Executive Office of Management and Budget (OMB) updates the areas at least annually. Information about what falls into a given MSA or NECMA can be found on the Executive Office of Management and Budget's website: http://www.whitehouse.gov/omb.

[90] 42 C.F.R. § 412.62(f)(1)(ii).

procedure numbered 51–100, this tiered compensation arrangement would not qualify for the deeming protection.

At the time the special rules of compensation were promulgated, percentage compensation was not considered to be set in advance and thus did not qualify for deeming protection. However, starting with the Phase II final rule, CMS policy is that percentage compensation can be considered set in advance. Although in the Phase III final rule CMS declined without explanation to extend the special rules on compensation to percentage compensation, a percentage compensation arrangement that met the requirements of the special rules on compensation nevertheless should be considered not to take into account the volume or value of referrals or other business generated, at least for the time period in which the Phase I guidance is applicable (pre-2020 final rule). There is no principled distinction between per click and percentage compensation that is in accord with the Phase I preamble guidance and special rules at (d)(2) and (d)(3).

In the 2020 final rule, CMS codified definitions of what does take into account the volume or value of referrals or other business generated. It concurrently amended sections (d)(2) and (d)(3) to say that these paragraphs do not apply for purposes of the new definitions of what takes into account the volume or value of referrals or other business generated. The preamble to the 2020 final rule is more explicit in saying that the new definitions supersede previous guidance[91] and that "[i]f compensation takes into account the volume or value of referrals or the volume or value of other business generated under [the new definitions] that determination is final. The special rules at § 411.354(d)(2) and (3) may not be applied to then deem the compensation not to take into account the volume or value of referrals or other business generated."[92]

Although the special rules at (d)(2) and (d)(3) are no longer applicable to direct compensation arrangements, the 2020 final rule states that they are built into the revised definition of indirect

---

[91] *See* 85 Fed. Reg. at 77537.

[92] *See id.* at 77538. *See also id.* at 77540 ("we are also clarifying in regulation text that, if compensation takes into account the volume or value of a physician's referrals to an entity or the volume or value of other business generated by a physician for an entity under final § 411.354(d)(5) or (6), no special rule, including those at § 411.354(d)(2) and (3), may be applied to reverse that determination").

compensation arrangements.[93] For example, suppose a physician-owned supplier contracts with a hospital to supply lithotripsy services to the hospital "under arrangements," and the compensation to the supplier is a per procedure fee that stays level regardless of the number of procedures. Such a compensation structure would not, by itself, cause physician owners of the supplier who refer lithotripsy procedures to the hospital to have an indirect compensation arrangement with the hospital.[94]

As another example of how the volume and value prohibition can operate differently in the context of a direct compensation arrangement versus an indirect compensation arrangement, consider percentage billing arrangements. Suppose a practice has a PSA with a hospital under which it is to perform oncology services and reassign to hospital the right to bill and collect for such services. The hospital wishes, however, to engage the practice to act as its billing agent due to the practice's expertise in billing oncology services. If the hospital wished to pay the practice a percentage of the revenue for the services billed, that would run afoul of the prohibition on taking into account the volume or value of DHS or other business generated. Because the payment would go to the physician group and the group's physician owners would stand in its shoes there would be a direct compensation arrangement under which there would be a positive correlation between a physician owner's referrals for DHS or other business generated and the amount of compensation paid to the group/physician standing in the shoes of the group. Now suppose the group forms an LLC for the express purpose of performing certain functions, including acting as a billing agent. In this case, there would be no direct compensation arrangement between the physician owners of the group and the hospital, and if the percentage of revenue was even

---

93 *See id.* at 77546 ("We are revising our regulations at § 411.354(c)(2)(ii) to effectively incorporate and apply the conditions of the special rules on unit-based compensation at the definitional level when determining whether an indirect compensation arrangement exists that must satisfy the requirements of an applicable exception in order to avoid the prohibitions of the physician self-referral law").

94 This is because, as noted above at section A.5.b.iv of this chapter, in the 2020 final rule CMS struck the language "regardless of whether individual unit of compensation satisfies the special rules on unit-based compensation" from the aggregate compensation test component of the definition of "indirect compensation arrangement."

and not tiered there would not be an indirect compensation arrangement on that basis.[95]

2. Special Rules on Compensation Arrangements (411.354(e)) Relating to the Signed, Written Agreement Requirement

a. *Signature Requirement*

Many of the exceptions that protect compensation arrangements require that there be a signed, written agreement. In the FY 2009 IPPS final rule, CMS promulgated a special rule that allowed parties a grace period for obtaining the needed signature(s) of a required written agreement. The grace period was 90 days from the beginning of the arrangement where the failure to get all necessary signatures was inadvertent, and 30 days from the beginning of the arrangement where the failure to obtain all necessary signatures was not inadvertent.[96] The grace period was for obtaining a necessary signature(s) only—there was no grace period for obtaining a written agreement.

Subsequently, CMS amended its rule to provide for a 90-day grace period irrespective of whether the failure to obtain all necessary signatures was inadvertent or not inadvertent.[97] The 2020 final rule also codified that the necessary signature can be satisfied through an electronic or other signature that is valid under applicable Federal or State law.[98]

b. *Written Agreement*

In the CY 2016 PFS rule, CMS reiterated its longstanding policy that the writing requirement may be satisfied through a compilation of writings. As CMS said:

> [T]here is no requirement under the physician self-referral law that an arrangement be documented in a single formal contract.

[95] There might or might not be an indirect compensation on some other basis, but the even percentage of revenue billing fee would not cause the arrangement to be an indirect compensation arrangement.

[96] The special rule was codified at 42 C.F.R. § 411.353(g). *See* 73 Fed. Reg. at 48751.

[97] *See* 80 Fed. Reg. at 71333, 71374.

[98] *See* 85 Fed. Reg. at 77591, 77667.

> Depending on the facts and circumstances of the arrangement and the available documentation, a collection of documents, including contemporaneous documents evidencing the course of conduct between the parties, may satisfy the writing requirement of the leasing exceptions and other exceptions that require that an arrangement be set out in writing.[99]

The 2020 final rule also instituted a 90-day grace period for the writing requirement.[100]

---

[99] *See* 80 Fed. Reg. at 71314-15.
[100] *See* 85 Fed. Reg. at 77591, 77677.

3
Definition of "Group Practice," Period of Disallowance, and Other Terms of Art and Concepts

OUTLINE

A. Definition of Group Practice (§ 411.352)

Under Stark, "group practice" is not a generic term for a multi-physician or other health care professional practice, but rather is a term of art that has many parts or requirements to its definition. "Group practice" status is required for the physician services exception[1] and is required, as a practical matter, for the in-office ancillary services (IOAS) exception.[2] "Group practice" status is important because group practices can compensate physicians in ways that other entities cannot (including physician groups that are not "group practices"). If a physician group no longer satisfies the definition of "group practice" (or never did), but compensates its physicians in a way that only a "group practice" may, the physician group's referrals for DHS or other business generated may be partially or completely tainted. Below are some of the requirements for a physician practice to qualify as a "group practice":

- Single legal entity (§ 411.352(a)—A group practice must be a single legal entity operating primarily for the purpose of being a physician group practice in any organizational form recognized by the State in which the group practice achieves its legal status (e.g., partnership, professional corporation (PC), limited liability company (LLC), foundation, nonprofit corporation, or faculty practice plan).[3] This does not mean that it cannot be owned by another entity (such as a hospital), but a physician practice will not qualify as a "group practice" if it is owned by another operating physician practice (regardless of whether the other practice is a "group practice").
- Two or more "members" (§ 411.352(b))—There must be two or more members. A member is a physician owner (direct or indirect) or an employee (full- or part-time). "Member of

[1] 42 C.F.R. § 411.355(a).

[2] 42 C.F.R. § 411.355(b). The IOAS exception can be used by a single physician practice, and, with some difficulty, can also be used by a multi-member physician practice that is not a "group practice."

[3] There is an exception to the single legal entity requirement for a practice operating in more than one State, provided that

> (1) The States in which the group practice is operating are contiguous (although each State need not be contiguous to every other State);
> (2) The legal entities are absolutely identical as to ownership, governance, and operation; and
> (3) Organization of the group practice into multiple entities is necessary to comply with jurisdictional licensing laws of the States in which the group practice operates.

42 C.F.R. § 411.352(a).

the group or member of a group practice" is defined at section 411.351 and does not include independent contractor physicians, who can be "physicians in the group practice."[4] As noted in Chapter 2, at A.5.b.i., the 2020 final rule excluded from the definition for ownership or investment interest titular ownership or investment interests. Therefore, when structuring an arrangement to create a "friendly PC" (which is usually done in conjunction with the creation of a management company), practitioners should keep in mind this exclusion if it is desired that the friendly PC qualify as a group practice. If the friendly PC is to be a "group practice" there must be at least two members, which could consist of two physician employees (one of whom could be the friendly PC "owner" if appropriate action is taken to make him or her an employee), or two physician owners (again, a nominal, friendly PC owner physician would not count as one), or at least one physician employee and one physician (non-titular) owner.[5]

- Range of care (§ 411.352(c))—Each member must furnish substantially the full range of patient care services[6] that the

---

4 Practitioners should be aware that when clients and others use the term "leased employee" they are often referring to what turns out to be independent contractors. The definition of "Member" specifically provides that "a leased employee is not a member of the group (unless the leased employee meets the definition of an 'employee' under this section)." See also the Phase III final rule, 73 Fed. Reg. at 51018, noting the differences between a "leased employee" and an actual employee. "Employee" is defined in section 411.351 in accordance with the common law/Internal Revenue Code meaning of the term.

5 "Member" also includes a "locum tenens" physician, which is a physician who temporarily stands in for the "regular physician" under certain circumstances and bills under the identifier of the regular physician. This begs the question why a locums tenens physician would be a "member" if the "regular physician" is only an independent contractor "physician in the group practice" to begin with. The answer seems to be that the Stark rules did not keep pace with a change in the statute. "Locum tenens physician" is defined in section 411.351 as incorporating the requirements for such a physician in section 1842(b)(6) of the Social Security Act, 42 U.S.C. § 1395u(b)(6). Until 2003, section 1842(b)(6) allowed reassignment to the employer of a physician but not to an entity that had only a contractual agreement.

6 "Patient care services" is defined at 42 C.F.R. § 411.351 as

> any task(s) performed by a physician in the group practice that address the medical needs of specific patients or patients in general, regardless of whether they involve direct patient encounters or generally benefit a particular practice. Patient care services can include, for example, the services of physicians who

physician routinely furnishes, including medical care, consultation, diagnosis, and treatment, through the joint use of shared office space, facilities, equipment, and personnel.

Unlike the "substantially all" test of § 411.352(d) (discussed below), here the requirement must be met with respect to each member. Therefore, group practices need to take care that all members who are performing services outside of the group (e.g., part-time employed physicians) are not performing a different range of services outside the group than they are performing inside the group. CMS has not issued guidance on how to quantify "substantially the full range" of patient care services.

- "Substantially All" test (§ 411.352(d))—Generally, "substantially all" (i.e., at least 75 percent) of the patient care services of the physicians who are members of the group must be furnished through the group and billed under a billing number assigned to the group, and the amounts received must be treated as receipts of the group. This is an aggregate test.

  Because a physician can be a member of, or otherwise work for, more than one physician practice, this requirement can be a problem for small group practices and care must be taken when structuring arrangements so that a practice does not fall out of compliance with the requirements for a "group practice." For example, suppose that Group 1 consists of two members, A and B, who work full time for the Group. The Group is considering employing or giving equity in the Group to a third, C. If physician C will not work exclusively for Group 1 but instead will continue to work a substantial amount of time for Group 2, Group 1 could fail to meet the "substantially all" test if physician C becomes a member, and/or Group 2 might fail the "substantially all" test, depending on the facts.

---

do not directly treat patients, such as time spent by a physician consulting with other physicians or reviewing laboratory tests, or time spent training staff members, arranging for equipment, or performing administrative or management tasks.

See also 63 Fed. Reg. at 1708 for discussion of the full range of services: test.

Patient care services must be measured by one of the following:

i. The total time each member spends on patient care services documented by any reasonable means (including, but not limited to, time cards, appointment schedules, or personal diaries).
ii. Any alternative measure that is reasonable, fixed in advance of the performance of the services being measured, uniformly applied over time, verifiable, and documented.

   One precise method, besides the total time approach, is to track all of the billable services performed by each member (the actual number of services approach) and simply determine whether 75 percent or greater of such services are performed on behalf of, and billed through, the group. Reportedly, CMS may also approve of the method whereby the group simply adds all of the percentages of billable services that were performed by each member on behalf of the group. Thus, under this methodology if Group has three members, and A performs 80 percent of her services through Group, B performs 90 percent of his services through Group, and C performs 60 percent of his services through Group, the resulting, unweighted average of the three is 76.67 percent, and the substantially all test would be met. Note that A and B might work relatively few hours and C might perform more services than A and B combined, so that if the total services of the three were tallied and compared to the aggregate number of services performed through Group, the percentage of services performed through Group could be well below 75 percent. Nevertheless, CMS may accept this methodology.[7]

The data used to calculate compliance with the substantially all test and related supportive documentation must be made available to the Secretary upon request.

[7] Note that using this simplified, unweighted average approach could only help a group, and not hurt it. That is, if the unweighted average approach were to produce a percentage below 75 percent but the actual number of services approach would yield a percentage of 75 percent or higher, the latter would govern.

The "substantially all" test does not apply to any group practice that is located solely in a Health Professional Shortage Area (HPSA). Also, for a group practice located outside of a HPSA, any time spent by a group practice member providing services in a HPSA is excluded from the "substantially all" test, which exclusion could assist the group practice in meeting the "substantially all" test.

Note that some group practices may devote some or all of their physician time to performing services at a hospital, through a personal services arrangement (PSA) under which the physicians reassign to the hospital their right to bill the professional services. Recall that the "substantially all" test requires that least 75 percent of the patient care services of the physicians who are members of the group must be furnished through the group and *billed under a billing number assigned to the group*. However, CMS takes the position that in the PSA situation described above, the billing requirement is met because the group would bill the hospital for its services, notwithstanding that the hospital would be the one billing Medicare and other payors.[8]

- Physician-patient encounters (§ 411.352(h))—Members of the group must personally conduct no less than 75 percent of the physician-patient encounters of the group practice.
- Compensation (§ 411.352(i))—A group practice is prohibited from paying its physicians base compensation that directly or indirectly takes into account the volume or value of referrals for DHS,[9] but may pay a share of "overall profits" (profit shares) and productivity bonuses that only indirectly take into account the volume or value of referrals for DHS. A productivity bonus may directly relate to the volume or value of the physician's referrals if the referrals are for services "incident to" the physician's personally performed services. There is no

---

[8] *See* discussion in Phase II, 69 Fed. Reg. at 16079-80.

[9] The 2020 final rule provided that, with respect to a physician's participation in a "value-based enterprise" (as defined in 411.351), profits from DHS that are directly attributable to such participation may be distributed to the participating physician. *See* 42 C.F.R. § 411.352(i)(3).

restriction, either in the base compensation or in profit shares/ productivity bonuses, on paying based on the volume or value of other business generated.

The group practice provisions on compensation provide safe harbors for methodologies that will be deemed not to directly relate to the volume or value of referrals for DHS for purposes of profit shares and productivity bonuses.

There is also special treatment afforded to profit shares paid to divisions or "pods" of five or more physicians. A pod of five or more physicians is treated as if it were a separate group practice for purposes of profit shares. Essentially, this allows a group practice to create pods in order to reward high referrers of DHS. For example, suppose a group practice has five orthopedic surgeons, three radiologists, and eight internists. It could choose to assign a percentage of all of its DHS revenue solely to the orthopedic surgeons. The DHS revenue that is accumulated in the orthopedists' pod would then be distributed amongst the orthopedists in a manner that does not take into account directly the volume or value of their referrals for DHS (e.g., distributed according to each surgeon's percentage of personally performed services as compared to the total of the five). Although the "pod rule" applies only to profit shares, it would seem that the same mechanism could be employed by a group practice with respect to productivity bonuses without running afoul of the prohibition of directly taking into account the volume or value of referrals of DHS. That is, given that CMS believes a pod of five or more physicians is sufficiently large to allow allocations of DHS to it without triggering a direct taking into account for purposes of profit shares, the same should be true with respect to productivity bonuses. Of course, the bonus payments to individual physicians within the pod would still need to be done in a manner that would not directly take into account the physicians' referrals for DHS.

The pod mechanism, if properly administered, provides a *safe harbor* for the distribution of profit shares. It should not be concluded that the allocation of DHS to a division of less than five physicians will necessarily result in the direct taking into account the volume or value of referrals; indeed the entire group practice may consist of less than five physicians.[10] The 2020 final rule amended the definition of "overall profits" in section 411.352(i) to say that overall profits means the profits derived from all the DHS of any component of the group that consists of at least five physicians (which may include all physicians in the group), and that if there are fewer than five physicians in the group, overall profits means the profits derived from all the DHS of the group.

The 2020 final rule also clarified that all DHS must be distributed according to the same methodology within a pod, although the methodology may differ from pod to pod. So, for example, Pod 1 could not distribute profit shares for radiology according to the proportion of personally performed services and distribute profit shares from radiation oncology on a per capita basis, but instead would have to have the same methodology for radiology as it would have for radiation oncology. However, Pod 2 might also have profits from radiology and radiation oncology allocated to it, and if so, could have a different (unified) methodology for distributing the profit shares from such DHS than Pod 1's (unified) methodology.

The compensation provisions of the group practice definition contain a safety valve, applicable to profit shares and productivity bonuses (and not base compensation) for those practices that can satisfy *both* of the following requirements: (1) revenues derived from DHS constitute less than five percent of the group practice's total revenues; and (2) the portion of those revenues distributed to *each* physician in the group constitutes five percent or less of his or her total compensation from the group.[11] Note that "total revenues" should be taken literally—one does not get to subtract DHS that was furnished pursuant to an arrangement that met an exception and then apply the five percent test only to DHS that did not meet an exception. If a group practice can satisfy both of the five percent requirements, the profit share distribution or productivity bonus will be deemed compliant (even if distribution methodology

---

[10] But if the group consists of more than five physicians, and there is a division of physicians that consists of less than five physicians, the onus would be on the group to show that the distribution of profit shares to this division did not directly take into account the volume or value of referrals.

[11] 42 C.F.R. § 411.352(i)(2)(C).

clearly takes into account directly the volume or value of referrals for DHS). The five percent de minimis test is rarely met, and it is not advisable to rely on it for planning purposes, but when faced with the fact that the profit share or productivity bonus distribution was not otherwise compliant, a practitioner should query the client to determine if, per chance, the test would be met.

B. Period of Disallowance

The period of disallowance is the period during which a physician may not refer DHS to an entity, and the entity may not bill Medicare or any other payor, due to a financial relationship between the physician (or an immediate family member of the physician) that does not meet the requirements of an exception.[12]

The commentary to the FY 2009 IPPS final rule posits that a compensation arrangement that implicates the statute must be protected by an exception at the inception of the arrangement —there is generally no opportunity to bring an arrangement into compliance retroactively.[13]

---

[12] The term "period of disallowance" first appeared in the CY 2008 PFS proposed rule. There, CMS stated that

> At this time, we are not making proposals for prescribing the period of disallowance for various types of noncompliance, but rather are seeking comments on how we might, to the extent practicable, set forth the period of disallowance for arrangements that implicate, but fail to satisfy the requirements of, one or more of the various exceptions. As a general matter, we believe that the statute contemplates that the period of disallowance should begin with the date that a financial arrangement failed to comply with the statute and the regulations and end with the date that the arrangement came into compliance or ended. However, in some instances it may not be clear when a financial arrangement has ended.

72 Fed. Reg. at 38183.

[13] *See* 73 Fed. Reg. 48703. This view was reaffirmed in the 2019 proposed rule, which distinguished attempts to turn back the clock with corrections of mistakes in the execution of the arrangement while the arrangement is still ongoing. 84 Fed. Reg. at 55811. As discussed below in this section, the 2020 final rule added new section 411.353(h)(1), which provides a 90-day grace period following the end of a compensation arrangement, in which the parties may reconcile all discrepancies in payments under the arrangement.

However, one should keep in mind that the beginning of a compensation arrangement does not necessarily equate to either the first payment that is made under the arrangement (indeed, payment may not occur for some time after the beginning, or may not occur at all), or the effective date of a written agreement (indeed, a written agreement may not be required by an applicable exception, or, if it is, it may not happen for some time or not occur ever). Likewise, the end of a compensation arrangement may not coincide with the termination of a written agreement (again, there may not be a written agreement). As CMS has said: "[i]n every case, a financial relationship begins and ends according to the conduct of the parties and the specific facts of the case."[14]

A helpful rule of thumb may be that a compensation arrangement begins or ends when the parties intend that it begins or ends, and such intention can be evidenced by the effective date of an agreement (oral or written), or the giving of remuneration (including services for which one expects to be compensated) by one party. With respect to an ownership or investment interest, State law may be instructive as to when that interest arises or terminates.

The analysis of when the period of disallowance ends is more or less straightforward depending on the particular exception involved. For example, if the parties to a space lease fail to have and sign a written lease, the period of disallowance could end when the parties come into compliance with an exception or the tenant vacates (voluntarily or otherwise) the premises. But consider the exception for nonmonetary compensation, which allows an entity to give nonmonetary compensation to a physician up to a certain prescribed limit. Suppose an entity provides no nonmonetary compensation to a physician for most of the year, and then, on December 15, provides nonmonetary compensation that is many times over the limit (e.g., a new car). What is the period of disallowance, i.e., the period for which the physician's referrals to the entity are tainted? Is the period January 1–December 31, December 15–December 31, December 15 to sometime beyond the end of the year? Similarly, what is the period of disallowance where an entity provides medical staff benefits to a physician that is day in and day out in accordance with the daily

---

[14] 73 Fed. Reg. at 48700.

limit under the exception, but one day goes slightly over the limit. Is the period of disallowance only for that day? What if, on a given day, the entity exceeds the limit by several times the daily limit? What is the period of disallowance for an entity that is generally in compliance with the rule that at least 75% of the DHS it furnishes is to patients who live in a rural area, but during one week it furnishes most of its DHS to patients who live in an urban area? Or is the provider even out of compliance with the exception in the first place?

Fortunately, entities that enter into the voluntary Self-Referral Disclosure Protocol (discussed infra at chapter 6 D.), may calculate on their own the period of disallowance (which CMS will accept unless it appears obviously incorrect to it), but they should keep in mind that the release they obtain from CMS at the end of the process is limited to the begin and end dates of the period they chose. Prior to the 2020 final rule, there were safe harbors through which parties could be assured that the period of disallowance had ended *no later than* a certain period, although they were free to take the position that the period of disallowance ended earlier.[15] The safe harbors provided that the period of disallowance ended no later than: (1) where the noncompliance is unrelated to compensation, the date that the financial relationship satisfies all of the requirements of an applicable exception; (2) where the noncompliance is due to the payment of excess compensation under the subject arrangement, the date on which the excess compensation is paid and the financial relationship satisfies all of the requirements of an applicable exception; and (3) where the noncompliance is due to a shortfall in the payment of compensation under the subject arrangement, the date on which all additional required compensation is paid, and the financial relationship satisfies all of the requirements of an applicable exception.[16] In the 2020 Final Rule, CMS made certain changes to its policy on determining the period of disallowance. It abolished the safe harbors announced in the FY 2009 IPPS final rule for when parties could be certain that the period of disallowance ended no later than a certain

[15] The safe harbors appeared at 42 C.F.R. § 411.353(c)(1). They were instituted by the FY 2009 inpatient prospective payment system (IPPS) final rule. *See* 73 Fed. Reg. at 48751.

[16] *See* 73 Fed. Reg. at 48700, 48751.

date. It also largely adopted the 2019 proposed rule's proposed policy that a new or modified arrangement springs into life based on an error in the execution of an arrangement, regardless of whether the mistake was on the part of only one of the parties, and whether the erroneous payment of compensation was intentional and/or deliberately hidden by one party from the other. CMS's position, that a compensation arrangement can be formed without the intention or knowledge of a party, or even against the will of the party, appears contrary to the plain language of the statute. The term "compensation arrangement" is defined in both the statute and regulations. The statute defines "compensation arrangement" as "any arrangement involving any remuneration between a physician (or an immediate family member of such physician) and an entity."[17] The regulations define "compensation arrangement" as an "arrangement involving remuneration, direct or indirect, between a physician (or a member of a physician's immediate family) and an entity."[18] Thus, both the statute and the regulations define "compensation arrangement" as an "arrangement" involving remuneration, but do not define "arrangement." However, the ordinary, common sense meaning of an "arrangement" is an agreement among two or more persons or entities, or in other words, a consensual relationship. Dictionary definitions are consistent with this meaning.[19] If parties agree to compensation at $140 per hour, that is the arrangement between them. If one party mistakenly pays the other $150 or $130 per hour, that does not change the basic fact that the arrangement was for $140 per hour. Likewise, if the parties discover the error and do not take appropriate action, that may result in a new arrangement (based on

---

[17] Section 1877(h)(1)(A) of the Social Security Act, 42 U.S.C. § 1395nn(h)(1)(A).

[18] 42 C.F.R. §411.354(c).

[19] For example, Cambridge Dictionary defines "arrangement" "as an agreement between two people or groups about how something happens or will happen." *See* https://dictionary.cambridge.org/us/dictionary/english/arrangement. Merriam-Webster defines "arrangement" as "an informal agreement or settlement especially on personal, social, or political matters." *See* https://www.merriam-webster.com/dictionary/arrangement. Collins Dictionary says "[a]n arrangement is an agreement that you make with someone to do something." https://www.collinsdictionary.com/us/dictionary/english/arrangement.

the intent of the parties[20]), but the mere fact, standing alone, that a mistake is made in the execution of the arrangement does not result in a new or modified arrangement.

In response to objections to the 2019 proposed rule's proposal that parties would have to, prior to the end of the arrangement, rectify an error in the execution of an arrangement (or else the supposed new or modified arrangement would kick in with the result that the parties would be out of compliance with an exception), CMS promulgated a grace period in the final rule. Section 411.353(h)(1), entitled "Special rule for reconciling compensation," provides:

> No later than 90 consecutive calendar days following the expiration or termination of a compensation arrangement, the entity and the physician (or immediate family member of a physician) that are parties to the compensation arrangement [may] reconcile all discrepancies in payments under the arrangement such that, following the reconciliation, the entire amount of remuneration for items or services has been paid as required under the terms and conditions of the arrangement[.]

Although the author has heard section 411.353(h)(1) described as a safe harbor, there is no indication in either its text or in the preamble to the 2020 final rule that meeting its requirements is merely optional, and that parties are free to argue that there has not been a modified or new compensation arrangement despite discrepancies in the agreed-upon compensation not being reconciled within 90 days following the expiration or termination of a compensation arrangement. Note that, in order for a party that has been underpaid by the other party (perhaps intentionally and surreptitiously) to avail itself of the protection of the final rule, it must recover all of the compensation owed it. Doing so may be either impossible or more expensive in terms of litigation costs than the amount owed. And the party

[20] If there is an error in the execution of an arrangement and the party that is underpaid discovers the error and does not take reasonable steps to recover what is owed, there is a new arrangement in the form of a gift (forgiveness of debt).

that has been underpaid may not, despite its best efforts, discover the underpayment within the 90-day period.

CMS has a legitimate interest in ensuring that parties to a Stark "financial relationship" are complying with the requirements of an applicable exception, and should not have to simply take a physician's or DHS's entity's word that remuneration that passed between the parties was unintended by the physician and/or the DHS entity. However, CMS can achieve that goal without exceeding its statutory authority, without causing unwarranted overpayment liability, and without putting the Medicare program at risk. Parties should endeavor, and CMS should allow them to correct the deviation from the arrangement (by ensuring that any overpayment in the remuneration is collected or any shortfall is paid) within 90 days of termination of the arrangement, but if they are not able to do that (either because the deviation has not been discovered during that time or the parties cannot resolve a dispute as to the proper amount of remuneration owed by one party to another), the entity that has furnished the DHS potentially at issue would be required to prove, upon appropriate demand, that the deviation did not result in a modified or new arrangement (or that if it did, there is no noncompliance). For example, if a hospital was shorted on the rent owed by a physician and did not discover it until after 90 days following the termination of the lease, it would be required to prove, in any enforcement action, that it did not agree to a modification of the rent. Further, if the hospital was unsuccessful in collecting all of the rent it was owed, it would be required to demonstrate that it expended efforts that were reasonable under the circumstances and that it did not intend to confer a gift upon the physician. The author recommends that entities include language similar to the following in their agreements with physicians, after the compensation methodology is set forth: "The compensation terms and conditions of this Agreement represent the true and correct compensation arrangement between the parties, and any inadvertent deviation from the terms and conditions by one or both parties, or any intentional deviation by one party, is ineffective to change the compensation arrangement between the parties. If a party has received or taken more remuneration than is owed under the terms and conditions of this Agreement, or has underpaid or delivered less remuneration than is owed under this Agreement, such party is not entitled to retain such additional remuneration and must return or deliver to the other party the remuneration that is owed upon discovery by either party of the shortfall in remuneration."

C. Other Terms of Art and Concepts

1. Burden of Proof

According to 42 C.F.R. § 411.353(c), the ultimate burden of proof (burden of persuasion) at each level of appeal is on the entity submitting the claim for payment to establish that the service was not furnished pursuant to a prohibited referral, but the burden of production on each issue at each level of appeal is initially on the claimant, but may shift to CMS or its contractors during the course of the appellate proceeding, depending on the evidence presented by the claimant.

2. Per-Click/Percentage Compensation Leases versus "Under Arrangements"

As noted above in the discussion of the revised definition of "entity,"[21] it may not always be clear when a party performs services that are billed as DHS, thus making the party an "entity." If there is any doubt as to whether an arrangement involving physician referrals is a lease arrangement or an "under arrangements" arrangement, most parties would prefer that it be considered a lease arrangement. That is because only a compensation exception would be needed and parties ought to be able to structure the compensation so that it does not run afoul of the per-click restriction or percentage compensation prohibition, whereas if the arrangement is considered an "under arrangements" arrangement, an ownership exception would be needed. However, in the case of lithotripsy, the preference is the opposite. Because CMS has (thus far) acquiesced in a court decision holding that lithotripsy is not DHS (even though it is furnished as an outpatient hospital service),

---

[21] *See supra* at Chapter 2, section A.3.

no ownership exception is required and parties may structure the compensation as a per-procedure fee or on a percentage-of-revenue basis (taking into account the other requirements of an applicable Stark exception and any AKS risk that may be presented by such a fee structure). CMS issued an FAQ shortly after the FY 2009 IPPS final rule, which reads in part: "Provided that a lithotripsy partnership is actually furnishing a service (or a package of services) to the hospital, and not merely leasing equipment over which the hospital would have dominion and control, the hospital may compensate the lithotripsy partnership using a per-unit or percentage-based compensation formula, as long as all of the requirements of a relevant exception are satisfied."[22]

3. Lithotripsy as Not DHS

Despite the fact that lithotripsy is most commonly furnished as an outpatient hospital service, and despite that, by statute, outpatient hospital services (and inpatient hospital services) are DHS, CMS does not consider lithotripsy to be DHS. This anomaly is a result of an erroneous district court decision, which favored select legislative "history" over the plain language of the statute.[23] The Government did not appeal the decision, and CMS has not exercised its rulemaking authority to overrule the decision. Instead, in the FY 2009 IPPS final rule, CMS said that it "presently" did not consider lithotripsy to be a DHS.[24] Although the court case involved extracorporeal lithotripsy, CMS has provided informal advice that it does not consider any form of lithotripsy to be DHS.

---

[22] *See* FAQ 9780, available at https://www.cms.gov/Medicare/Fraud-and-Abuse/PhysicianSelfReferral/Downloads/FAQs-Physician-Self-Referral-Law.pdf.

[23] *Am. Lithotripsy Soc. v. Thompson*, 215 F. Supp. 2d 23 (D.D.C. 2002).

[24] 73 Fed. Reg. at 48719 (middle column).

4
Exceptions, Waivers, and Other Relief

OUTLINE

Although Stark generally prohibits a physician from referring DHS to an entity with which the physician (or his or her immediate family member) has a financial relationship, there are numerous exceptions that enable financial relationships to be formed and referrals to be made. Because Stark is a strict liability statute, it is essential to meet every element of an exception. Failure to comply with all the elements of an exception will mean that exception is not available, and if there is a prohibited financial relationship that does not satisfy any exception, any referral of DHS to an entity with which the physician has the prohibited financial relationship will result in a violation (unless there is an applicable waiver).

It is not necessary to meet more than one exception to protect a financial relationship and parties need not declare ahead of time (i.e., prior to a financial arrangement coming into question) which exception they believe protects the financial relationship. Of course, parties to a planned financial relationship should structure the relationship with a particular exception or exceptions in mind. And to do that, the parties or their counsel must have a good understanding of the Stark exceptions. Bear in mind that a physician who refers DHS to an entity may have more than one financial relationship with that entity, and each financial relationship needs to meet an exception (which is not to say that the same exception will be met or even applicable).[1]

The exceptions to Stark can be broken into three main categories: (1) those that protect services performed under certain circumstances, (2) those that protect ownership or investment interests, and (3) those that protect compensation arrangements.

What follows is a discussion of the more notable exceptions in each of the three categories noted above. As a caveat, there are many other exceptions that are not discussed in any depth below, but practitioners should be familiar with all of the exceptions, even the ones that are of limited use, lest they overlook one that could be used to structure an arrangement or to avoid making a self-disclosure or to defend against a False Claims Act (FCA) action. Another important caveat is that for the sake of convenience and saving space, *not all of the requirements of a given exception may be mentioned, and some requirements that are mentioned are not fully stated.* There is no substitute for consulting the actual wording of the exceptions when

---

[1] For example, suppose a physician has a long term office space lease with a hospital and also is paid by the hospital for taking emergency call. The office space rental might be protected by the exception for space leases and the call arrangement might be protected by the exception for personal service arrangements or the exception for fair market value compensation.

performing a Stark analysis, particularly because the exceptions are amended (or added to) from time to time.

In addition to the exceptions, as that term is commonly understood, this chapter covers the so-called "section 353 exceptions" and the Secretary's authority to waive requirements of the Stark law.

A. The Exceptions

1. Service-Based Exceptions (§ 411.355)

As the name implies, the service-based exceptions, also known as general exceptions, protect certain designated health services that are performed under certain conditions, and generally without regard to the nature of the financial relationship (ownership/investment interest or compensation arrangement) between the referring physician and the entity. If the requirements of a service-based exception are satisfied, *the prohibition on referrals* does not apply to referrals of the relevant services. The fundamental difference between the service-based exceptions and the compensation/ownership exceptions is this—a service-based exception protects only a service, leaving the underlying financial relationship intact, but where a compensation arrangement or ownership/investment interest is protected by a compensation exception or an ownership exception, as applicable, it is as if the compensation arrangement or ownership/investment interest did not exist, so that all designated health services referred by the physician to the entity are protected. For this reason, when structuring an arrangement to meet the service-based exception, practitioners should keep in mind the underlying financial relationship and the scope of designated health services potentially referred by the physician in case that financial relationship rears its ugly head in another arrangement between the parties in which the physician refers other DHS to the entity that are not protected by a service-based exception.

Example: Group Practice pays Employed Physician above fair market value. Employed Physician refers DHS within Group Practice that is protected by the service-based in-office ancillary services exception, which does not have a fair market value requirement. However, Employed Physician's compensation from Group Practice also creates an indirect compensation arrangement with Hospital (and referrals to a hospital are not protected by the in-office ancillary services exception). Because Employed Physician is paid above fair market value, the exception for indirect compensation arrangements cannot be satisfied.

Example: Physician refers Medicare patient to a freestanding imaging center in which Physician's spouse has an ownership interest. Physician's ownership interest does not meet the requirements of an ownership/investment exception. Patient resides in a rural area and the referral meets all of the other conditions of the intra-family rural referrals service-based exception. The referral is protected by the exception but the ownership interest of Physician's immediate family member is not. If Physician refers a Medicare patient who resides in an urban area to the imaging center, and the imaging center bills for the service, a Stark violation results.

Where the referring physician has an ownership interest in a DHS entity, if a service-based exception cannot be met, it is unlikely that there will be an applicable ownership/investment exception.

---

a. In-Office Ancillary Services (§ 411.355(b))

The in-office ancillary services (IOAS) exception is perhaps the most important Stark exception. The exception protects referrals within a "group practice," including referrals from owners of the group practice. Because "group practice" status is necessary as a practical matter to take advantage of the IOAS exception, and because a group practice is permitted to compensate physicians in ways that other entities (including physician practices that do not meet the definition of a "group practice") cannot, there is a strong incentive to rely on the IOAS exception along with a certain danger in doing so. That is, if a practice compensates its physicians in accordance with the favorable provisions of the group practice definition (e.g., it pays its physicians profit shares and/or productivity bonuses in a manner that indirectly takes into account the volume or value of referrals), but fails to meet, or maintain compliance with, the "group practice" definition, all of its referrals for DHS within the practice may be tainted. For that reason, some group practices will purposefully structure their compensation arrangements with their physicians to meet the more stringent requirements of a compensation exception. Of course, a compensation exception will not protect referrals for DHS from physician owners of the practice, but this conservative approach could limit the amount of tainted DHS subject to repayment should the practice not meet the definition of "group practice;" moreover, the group may have no owners or the owners may not refer DHS.

There are essentially three requirements to the IOAS exception, relating to: (1) who is performing/supervising the DHS, (2) where the DHS is performed, and (3) who is billing for the DHS.[2]

First, the services must be furnished personally by (1) the referring physician, i.e., self-performed, (2) a physician who is a member of the same group practice as the referring physician, or (3) an individual who is supervised by either the referring physician or another physician in the group practice.[3] If supervision is relied upon to satisfy the IOAS exception performance element, the appropriate level of supervision must be used. Although the statute uses the language "directly supervised," which may appear to invoke the term of art "direct supervision," CMS takes the position that whatever level of supervision is required under the Medicare payment rules is the level of supervision required for purposes of the IOAS exception.[4]

Second, for the location element, the DHS must be furnished in (1) the same building where the referring physician or another member

---

2 42 C.F.R. § 411.355(b)(1).

3 The statute lists the referring physician as one of the categories of individuals who may personally furnish the DHS, which begs the question of why that is the case, given that a physician's personally performed service is not a referral in the first place. The answer is that the rule that a physician's personally performed service is not a referral was instituted post-enactment by CMS. In the regulatory version of the IOAS exception, CMS elected to parrot the language of the statute notwithstanding its promulgation of the rule concerning personally performed services. *See* 42 C.F.R. § 411.355(b)(1)(i).

4 Regulation 42 C.F.R. § 410.32 defines the three levels of supervision (general, direct, and personal), and specifies the supervision level required for certain diagnostic tests. The required supervision level for other diagnostic tests and for therapeutic services is set forth in other regulations, manual instructions, and on CMS's website.

of the group practice regularly practices,[5] (2) in a centralized building that is used by the referring physician or the group practice for some or all of its clinical laboratory services, or (3) a centralized building that is used by the referring physician or the group practice for some or all of the group's DHS. When considering the location where services under the IOAS exception can be performed, both types of buildings, same or centralized, are given special definitions by the Stark Regulations. The "same building" is a structure or combination of structures sharing a single postal street address, but does not include mobile trailers, vans, or vehicles as is permissible under the centralized building definition.[6] A "centralized building" is all or part of a building (including a mobile trailer, van, or vehicle) that is owned or leased by the group practice full-time, i.e., no time-sharing occurs, and is used exclusively by the group practice.[7]

A special rule exists for home-care physicians under the IOAS exception.[8] For a referring physician who principally treats patients in the patient's private home, the same building requirement is met if the referring physician, or a qualified person accompanying the referring physician, provides the designated health services contemporaneously with a physician service that is not DHS in the patient's home. A private home does not include a nursing home, long-term care, or other facility or institution, though a patient may have a private home in such a place.

There is also a special provision, at section 411.355(b)(5), relating to the location requirement, that was added in the Phase I final rulemaking. It provides that a DHS is "furnished" "in the location where the service is actually performed upon a patient or where an item is dispensed to a patient in a manner that is sufficient to meet the applicable Medicare payment and coverage rules." This language was added

---

[5] The requirements for meeting the "same building" test are somewhat involved and are set forth in three alternative sets of criteria at 42 C.F.R. § 411.355(b)(2)(i).

[6] 42 C.F.R. § 411.351 (Same building). Because mobile trailers do not qualify as a "same building," and because MRIs and other imaging services can and are delivered through mobile units, some entities will take steps through various means to incorporate a mobile unit into a building (such as designing the building in the first instance to allow the mobile unit to be driven into the loading dock and attached to the building).

[7] 42 C.F.R. § 411.351 (Centralized building).

[8] 42 C.F.R. § 411.355(b)(6).

ostensibly to accommodate drugs or other items such as prosthetic devices that are furnished in the physician's office but used at home. The 1998 proposed rule would have taken a stricter approach, saying that "any item that is given to a patient but is meant to be used at home or outside the physician's office, or any item that is delivered to the patient's home, has not been 'furnished' in the physician's office."[9] Paragraph (b)(5) is perhaps inartfully drafted, but should not be read as broadly as it might appear, or otherwise the same building and centralized building location restrictions would be meaningless.[10]

Third, the DHS must be billed by: (1) the physician performing or supervising the service; (2) the group practice of which the performing or supervising physician is a member; (3) the group practice if the supervising physician is a "physician in the group practice" as that phrase is defined in 42 C.F.R. § 411.351; (4) an entity wholly owned by the performing or supervising physician or such physician's group practice; or (5) an independent third-party billing company acting as an agent for one of the foregoing.

In addition to the above three basic requirements, there is also a disclosure requirement for certain imaging services.[11] For MRI, computerized tomography (CT), and positron emission tomography (PET) services, the referring physician must provide written notice to the patient at the time of the referral that the patient may receive such imaging services from another physician or supplier. The written notice must include a list of at least five other suppliers that provide the service for which the patient is being referred and which are located within a twenty-five-mile radius of the referring physician's office. If there are fewer than five such suppliers, then the list must include all suppliers within the twenty-five-mile radius of the referring physician's office.

Finally, it should be noted that whereas the IOAS exception protects the great majority of DHS referred within a group practice, it cannot be used for most durable medical equipment (DME). The DME that can be protected by the IOAS exception are limited to canes, crutches,

---

[9] *See* 63 Fed. Reg. at 1695.

[10] CMS issued an FAQ in 2018 to explain its view of paragraph (b)(5). *See* https://www.cms.gov/Medicare/Fraud-and-Abuse/PhysicianSelfReferral/Downloads/FAQs-Physician-Self-Referral-Law.pdf.

[11] 42 C.F.R. § 411.355(b)(7).

walkers, folding manual wheelchairs, blood glucose monitors that meet certain conditions,[12] and certain infusion pumps.[13] Note that the exclusion is for "DME" and not for durable medical equipment, prosthetics, orthotics and supplies (DMEPOS). Prosthetics, orthotics and supplies are covered by the IOAS exception.

i. Physician Services (§ 411.355(a))

This exception protects professional physician services if furnished personally by another physician who is a member of the referring physician's group practice, or under the supervision of another physician who is a member of the group practice.[14] Although not as versatile as the in-office ancillary services exception, the physician services exception does have one advantage over the IOAS exception, namely, there is no location requirement. However, although there is no location requirement per se in the exception, only physicians in the group practice who are members (i.e., employee or owner) benefit from the lack of the location requirement. That is because an independent contractor is a "physician in the group practice" only when he or she is performing services on the group's premises.[15]

Example: Employed Physician in Group Practice performs a read of an X-ray that was referred to Employed Physician from another physician in Group Practice. Employed Physician performs the read while at home. The read would not be protected by the IOAS exception but may be protected by the physician services exception. If the physician were instead an independent contractor for the group, neither exception would be satisfied.

---

ii. Academic Medical Centers (§ 411.355(e))

For purposes of this exception an academic medical center (AMC) consists of (1) an accredited medical school or an accredited academic

[12] 42 C.F.R. § 411.355(b)(4).
[13] 42 C.F.R. § 411.355.
[14] 42 C.F.R. § 411.355(a).
[15] *See* 42 C.F.R. § 411.351 (definition of "physician in the group practice").

hospital; and (2) one or more affiliated hospitals (which may be the accredited academic hospital for purpose of (1)) in which a majority of the physicians on the medical staff consists of physicians who are faculty members[16] and a majority of all hospital admissions is made by physicians who are faculty members; and (3) one or more faculty practice plans affiliated with the medical school, the affiliated hospital(s), or the accredited academic hospital.[17] The exception imposes requirements on the physician, including certain fair market value requirements, as well as on the AMC.

iii. Intra-Family Rural Referrals

CMS promulgated the exception for intra-family rural referrals to address access to care issues for Medicare patients in rural areas, and specifically where the only DHS entity available to furnish services to a Medicare patient is one that has a financial relationship with an immediate family member of the referring physician. The requires that (1) the referred patient must reside in a rural area, (2) no other person or entity is available to provide the services in a timely manner within 25 miles or 45 minutes' transportation time from the patient's residence, (3) no other person or entity is available to provide the services in a timely manner where the patient resides, and (4) the referring physician or the physician's immediate family member makes reasonable inquiries to determine if any other person or entity is available to provide the service within 25 miles or 45 minutes' transportation time.

---

[16] A faculty member is a physician who is either on the faculty of the affiliated medical school or on the faculty of one or more of the educational programs at the accredited academic hospital. Faculty from any affiliated medical school or accredited academic hospital education program may be aggregated, and residents and non-physician professionals need not be counted. Any faculty member may be counted, including courtesy and volunteer faculty. For purposes of determining whether the majority of physicians on the medical staff consists of faculty members, the affiliated hospital must include or exclude all individual physicians with the same class of privileges at the affiliated hospital (for example, physicians holding courtesy privileges). *See* 42 C.F.R. § 411.355(e)(2)(iii).

[17] 42 C.F.R. § 411.355(e)(2)(i) – (iii).

b. *Other Service-Based Exceptions*

The remaining service-based exceptions are: (1) services furnished by certain managed care organizations (or their contractors or subcontractors) to enrollees (§ 411.355(c)); implants furnished by an ASC (§ 411.355(f)); EPO and other dialysis-related drugs (411.355(g)); preventive screening tests and vaccines (§ 411.355(h)); and eyeglasses and contact lenses following cataract surgery (§ 411.355(i)).

2. Ownership/Investment Interest Exceptions (§ 411.356)

The ownership and investment interest exceptions protect ownership or investment interests in entities.[18] In contrast to the service-based exceptions and compensation exceptions, there are very few ownership/investment exceptions—only five to be exact. Three of the five are rarely used.[19] That leaves the rural provider exception, and the whole hospital exception.

a. *Publicly Traded Securities (§ 411.356(a))*

The exception requires that (1) the investment be in securities that may be purchased on terms generally available to the public; (2) the securities must be listed on the New York Stock Exchange, the American Stock Exchange, or certain other specified exchanges; and (3) the investment be in a corporation that had shareholder equity exceeding $75 million at the end of the corporation's most recent fiscal year or on average during the previous three fiscal years.[20] Alternatively, the exception may be satisfied by ownership of shares in a regulated investment company as defined in section 851(a) of the Internal Revenue Code of 1986, if the company had, at the end of its most recent fiscal year, or on average during the previous 3 fiscal years, total assets exceeding $75 million.

---

[18] 42 C.F.R. § 411.356.

[19] The three are the exceptions for publicly traded securities (§ 411.356(a)), mutual funds (§ 411.356(b)), and hospitals in Puerto Rico (§ 411.356(c)(2)).

[20] As a cautionary note, 'stockholder equity" is defined as "the difference in value between a corporation's total assets and total liabilities." 42 C.F.R. § 411.356(a)(1). This means that even large companies with stock valued well in excess of $75 million may not qualify for the exception if they also have large debt.

b. *Rural Provider (§411.356(b))*

Ownership or investment interests are permissible in a rural provider that furnishes DHS in a rural area, as that term is defined in the regulations.[21] Despite its name, the exception protects ownership/investment interests in suppliers as well as providers of services. A rural provider is an entity that furnishes at least 75 percent of its DHS to residents of a rural area. A rural area is any area that is not an urban area.[22] The exception does not specify, and CMS has not provided any guidance, on the period of time for which the entity must meet the 75 percent requirement.[23]

The restrictions placed by the Patient Protection and Affordable Care Act (ACA) of 2010[24] on the use of the rural provider exception by hospitals are discussed below with respect to the "whole hospital" exception.

c. *Hospital Ownership*

Ownership of a whole hospital provides another exception from the Stark referral and billing prohibitions.[25] The so-called "whole hospital" exception requires the referring physician to be authorized to perform services at the hospital, and the ownership or investment interest to be in the entire hospital, not just a distinct part or department of the hospital, i.e., the whole hospital, not just a line of service.

---

[21] 42 C.F.R. § 411.356(c)(1). *See* Section B.1.g. for the definition of rural area.

[22] 42 C.F.R. § 411.351 (definition of rural area). Urban area is defined at 42 C.F.R. § 412.62(f)(1)(ii).

[23] Is the period of time measured on a month-by-month basis, on a calendar year, or 12-month basis? If a provider meets the 75 percent requirement for each month throughout a year, but fails to meet it during two weeks in August, are referrals from the provider's owners tainted during those two weeks? Would referrals be tainted if the provider met the 75% requirement for every month during the year except for one month? Would the answer depend on whether the non-rural referrals during that month did or did not cause the provider to fail the 75% requirement on an aggregate basis for the year? And what would be the period of disallowance? For example, suppose for the sake of argument the provider must meet the 75% requirement for each month during a calendar year, but fails to meet it for October of a given year—are the referrals from the owners tainted for only October, or for October through the end of the year, or for the entire year?

[24] Section 6001 of the Patient Protection and Affordable Care Act, Pub. L. No. 111-148 (codified at 42 U.S.C. § 1395nn(i)).

[25] 42 C.F.R. § 411.356(c)(3).

Note that the ownership must be in the hospital itself, and not in an entity such as a home health agency that is owned by the hospital.[26]

The ACA significantly changed the requirements by which a hospital can qualify for the whole hospital exception or for the rural provider exception.[27] Essentially, the ACA abolished, prospectively, the whole hospital exception, and the use of the rural provider exception by hospitals, while grandfathering certain hospitals and imposing certain requirements that grandfathered hospitals must continue to meet order to maintain grandfathered status.

In order to be grandfathered, a hospital must have had physician ownership as of March 23, 2010, and a Medicare provider agreement in effect on December 31, 2010. CMS has clarified that this latter requirement is met if the provider agreement was issued after December 31, 2010, provided that the provider agreement letter contains an effective date of on or before December 31, 2010.[28] The hospital cannot have been converted from an ambulatory surgical center into a hospital on or after March 23, 2010.

In addition, the ACA placed restrictions and requirements on grandfathered hospitals, all of which appear in the regulations at 411.362. What follows are some (not all) of the restrictions and requirements.

i. Restrictions Related to Physician Ownership (§ 411.362(b)(1), (b)(4))

The percentage of permitted physician ownership cannot at any time be greater than the percentage that existed on March 23, 2010.[29] Originally, CMS took the position that the ownership or investment interests of non-referring physicians "need not" be considered when calculating the baseline physician ownership level and the physician

---

[26] In response to commenters that objected to CMS's interpretation that the exception applies only to services furnished by the hospital and not to services furnished by other providers owned by the hospital, CMS noted that the commenters ignored the language in the statutory exception, "provided by a hospital." *See* 69 Fed. Reg. at 16084-85.

[27] Section 6001 of the ACA.

[28] *See* 75 Fed. Reg. at 72242.

[29] The number of physician owners may be greater at various times than the number on March 23, 2010, but the percentage of ownership cannot increase. *See* 75 Fed. Reg. at 72249.

ownership level thereafter.[30] However, CMS subsequently reversed course, and requires that the baseline physician investment percentage level and the percentage at any time thereafter include direct and indirect ownership and investment interests held by a physician if he or she satisfies the definition of "physician" in section 1861(r) of the Social Security Act and in § 411.351, regardless of whether the physician refers patients to the hospital (and regardless of whether the physician even practices medicine).[31] CMS did not characterize its revised policy as a clarification or give any indication in the final rule that the revision was retroactive, so query whether hospitals that took advantage of CMS's original policy by not counting the ownership/investment interests of non-referring physicians who were added to the ownership rolls after March 23, 2010, may continue to exclude their interests after the effective date of the final rule (January 1, 2016).

In addition, the ACA placed the following conditions related to physician ownership in order for the hospital to receive grandfathering protection: (1) ownership or investment interests are not offered to physicians on more favorable terms than non-physicians; (2) the hospital does not, directly or indirectly, provide loans or financing for any investment in the hospital by a physician owner or investor; (3) the hospital does not, directly or indirectly, guarantee a loan, make a loan payment, or otherwise subsidize a loan of any physician or group of physicians related to the acquisition of an ownership or investment interest in the hospital; (4) returns are distributed to each owner or investor in an amount that is directly proportional to the ownership or investment interest (no favoritism); (5) physician owners and investors do not have a guaranteed receipt of or a right to acquire any other business interests related to the hospital; and (6) physician owners or investors are not afforded the opportunity to purchase or lease any property controlled by the hospital on terms more favorable than offered to non-physician owners or investors.

---

[30] *See* 75 Fed. Reg. at 72250. Query whether a grandfathered hospital could include the ownership/investment interests of non-referring physicians in order to maximize the baseline percentage but then subsequently not include the ownership/investment interests of added non-referring physicians so as not to exceed the baseline percentage.

[31] *See* 80 Fed. Reg. at 71337-40.

ii. Restrictions on Aggregate Number of Operating Rooms, Procedure Rooms, and Beds (§ 411.362(b)(2), (c))

The aggregate number of licensed operating rooms, procedure rooms, and beds cannot be increased from what existed as of March 23, 2010, unless an exception is granted (see below).

The ACA authorized the Secretary to grant exceptions to the expansion limits through the regulatory process, which would include the opportunity for community input. The regulations establishing the expansion exception process were promulgated through the CY 2012 Hospital Outpatient Prospective Payment System Final Rule.[32] Generally, hospitals are eligible to submit an application for expansion once every two years from the date of CMS's decision on the hospital's most recent application.[33] The procedure itself requires submission of a written request, by mail or electronically, to CMS to qualify for the exception, along with certain documentation and a certification that all information is true and correct.[34] The hospital must publicly disclose its expansion request until CMS makes a decision. Additionally, interested individuals and/or entities within the hospital's community may provide input to CMS on the proposed expansion.

The criteria for the submission depend upon whether the hospital is an "applicable hospital" or a "high Medicaid facility."

An applicable hospital is a grandfathered hospital that meets the following criteria: (1) is located in a county that has a percentage population increase that is at least 150 percent of the percentage population increase in the state where the hospital is located during the most recent five-year period; (2) have its percentage of annual Medicaid inpatient admissions be equal to or greater than the average percentage of such admissions for all other hospitals in the county during the most recent fiscal year; (3) not discriminate against beneficiaries of federal health care programs; (4) be located in a state in which the average bed capacity in the state is less than the national

---

32 76 Fed. Reg. 74122 (Nov. 30, 2011). The expansion regulations can be found at 42 C.F.R. § 411.362(c) (2011).

33 42 C.F.R. § 411.362(c)(1).

34 42 C.F.R. § 411.362(c)(4).

average bed capacity; and (5) have an average bed occupancy rate that is greater than the average bed occupancy rate in the state where the hospital is located during the most recent fiscal year.

A high Medicaid facility is one that meets the following criteria:[35] (1) the hospital is not the sole hospital in its area; and (2) with respect to each of the 3 most recent 12-month periods for which data are available as of the date the hospital submits its request, the hospital has an annual percent of total inpatient admissions under Medicaid that is estimated to be greater than such percent with respect to such admissions for any other hospital located in the county in which the hospital is located; and (3) the hospital does not discriminate against beneficiaries of Federal health care programs.

By statute, with respect to an applicable hospital that is granted an exception, any increase in the aggregate number of operating rooms or procedure rooms cannot exceed 200 percent of the hospital's aggregate baseline, and may occur only in facilities on the main campus of the applicable hospital.[36] The statute does not specify such limits on high Medicaid facilities, and originally, CMS took the position that it made sense to impose the same limits on high Medicaid facilities and did so through the CY 2012 OPPS final rule.[37] However, in a 2020 final rule, CMS removed these limits on high Medicaid facilities, citing the Patients over Paperwork initiative.[38] Because there is no limit on the expansion or requirement that the expansion take place on the main campus, it is possible for a hospital that qualifies as a high Medicaid facility to acquire or build a facility far away from the main campus and obtain provider-based status for the "remote location," which facility would be operated under the same provider agreement as the high-Medicaid facility and essentially nullify Congressional intent to limit the expansion of physician-owned hospitals. Moreover, CMS has taken the position that a high Medicaid facility does not have to meet the criteria prescribed for such status for any length of time.[39]

---

[35] 42 C.F.R. § 411.362(c)(3).

[36] Section 1877(i)(3)(D) of the Social Security Act, 42 U.S.C. § 1395nn(i)(3)(D).

[37] *See* 76 Fed. Reg. at 74524.

[38] 85 Fed. Reg. 85886, 86255-59 (Dec. 29, 2020). The cited justification may seem like a make-weight, or paper weight, reason to some.

[39] *See* 85 Fed. Reg. at 86257.

iii. Disclosure Requirements (§ 411.362(b)(3), (5))

Disclosure requirements include: (1) the hospital must annually provide reports to the Secretary of HHS concerning the identity of each physician owner or investor in the hospital along with the nature and extent of the ownership or investment interest; (2) the hospital must have procedures in place requiring any referring physician who is an owner or investor in the hospital to disclose to patients the nature of that physician's ownership or investment interest with enough advance notice to allow the patient to make a meaningful decision about the receipt of care; and (3) the hospital must disclose the physician ownership or investment interests on its public website or in any public advertisement.[40]

If the hospital admits a patient and does not have any physician available on hospital premises to provide services during all hours when the hospital is providing services to the patient, the hospital must disclose such information to the patient and before providing services to the patient, it must receive a signed acknowledgement from the patient stating that the patient understands that a physician may not be present during all hours that services are furnished to the patient.

Where a grandfathered hospital falls out of compliance with the requirements for grandfathered status (e.g., it increases its baseline percentage of physician ownership or increases its aggregate total number of beds, operating rooms, and procedure rooms without being granted an exception), it is unknown what the effect will be. Will the whole hospital exception or the hospital's ability to use of the rural provider exception be permanently lost (certainly a permissible interpretation) or only for a period of time?

---

40 CMS has a special form for self-disclosures of the failure to make this disclosure. *See:* https://www.cms.gov/Medicare/Fraud-and-Abuse/PhysicianSelfReferral/Downloads/Disclosures-Noncompliance-Instructions.pdf. According to the instructions, CMS had received numerous self-disclosures of noncompliance with this requirement. Reportedly the money penalties have been slight, and no hospital has lost its ability to rely on the whole hospital exception solely because of noncompliance with this disclosure requirement.

3. Compensation Exceptions

The largest group of exceptions are the exceptions for compensation arrangements (commonly called compensation exceptions). Some were created by statute, but most have been created by regulation. To reiterate, where an arrangement is protected by a compensation exception it is as if the compensation arrangement does not exist. A compensation arrangement may fit into no exception, one exception, or more than one exception.

There are certain requirements that are present in several or many of the compensation exceptions, such as: compensation that is set in advance, fair market value, and compensation not determined in a manner that takes into account the volume or value of referrals for DHS or other business generated; a signed written agreement for a term of a year or more; and commercial reasonableness. Four of the exceptions disallow protection for so-called percentage or per-click lease arrangements.[41]

However, the exceptions are numerous enough and varied enough in their coverage that there is a good amount of difference in their requirements, so one must be careful not to miss slight differences. For example, the exception for bona fide employment arrangements does not require a written agreement or that the compensation be set in advance, and requires that the compensation not be determined in a manner that takes into account the volume or value of referrals for DHS only. There is no prohibition on taking into account the volume or value of referrals for other business generated between the parties. The exception for indirect compensation arrangements does not have a set in advance requirement. And whereas most of the exceptions that do not allow compensation to be determined in a manner that takes into account the volume or value of other business generated and/or referrals for DHS do not distinguish between direct and indirect takings into account, the exceptions for donations of EHR and cybersecurity disallow only direct takings into account. Also, whereas many of the exceptions pertain to compensation between any entity

41 The four exceptions are the exceptions for space leases (§ 411.357(a)); equipment leases (§ 411.357(b)); fair market value compensation (§ 411.357(l)); and indirect compensation arrangements (§ 411.357(p)).

and a physician or immediate family member, some are applicable only to hospitals or other entities.

Rather than proceed alphabetically through section 411.357, the discussion below is organized by grouping together exceptions that are at least somewhat related to each other.

a. *Exceptions for Office Space and Equipment Leases (§ 411.357(a) and (b)); Timeshare Arrangements (§ 411.357(y))*

i. Office Space and Equipment Leases (§ 411.357(a) and (b))

The two exceptions for lease or rental arrangements are largely identical, aside from the fact that one is for space and one is for equipment. These exceptions apply to leasehold interests, unlike the exception for timeshare arrangements (§ 411.357(y)) which specifically does not apply to leasehold interests. The exceptions require that (1) there is a written agreement signed by the parties that specifies the premises or equipment covered; (2) the agreement has a term of at least one year; (3) the amount of space or equipment rented is reasonable and necessary for a legitimate business purpose and is used exclusively by the lessee when the lessee is using the space or equipment; (4) the amount of the rental charge is set in advance and is consistent with fair market value; (5) the rental charge is not determined in a manner that takes into account the volume or value of referrals or other business generated between the parties or using a formula that relates to a percentage of revenue or per-click uses; and (6) the agreement is commercially reasonable.

The lease exceptions permit a holdover period of unlimited duration.

As noted above, the exceptions require a term of at least a year. It is common for parties to provide for an automatic renewal provision in the lease, and also a means for increasing the compensation for the renewal term(s), such as indexing the compensation to the CPI-U. CMS takes the position that the compensation must be consistent with fair market value throughout the term of the lease. CMS has warned that parties need to be careful that the compensation does not fall out of fair market value, a warning which should be especially heeded where the parties' arrangement is in the later years of a multi-year original term, or is several years removed from the original one-year term, either due to automatic renewals or a holdover. A built-in inflation adjustment generally is a good idea but is not foolproof. The lease exceptions require that compensation be "consistent with" fair market value, which CMS takes to mean compensation that is neither lower nor higher than the range of fair market value. Slight movements toward one end or the other of the range of that occur in a year or two, despite the use of a built-in adjustment, can be magnified over several years. The problem can be especially acute if there is an adjustment that assumes inflation but the market for space or equipment is in a downturn.

Prior to the FY 2009 IPPS final rule, per-click (unit of service) and percentage-based compensation arrangements were permissible with regard to rental agreements. This meant that a rental amount could be tied to the actual use of the space or equipment. However, after the effective date of that rule (which was delayed for one year), per-click arrangements became prohibited insofar as the lessor would receive a per-click payment for use of the space or equipment by the lessee in furnishing services referred by the lessor to the lessee. Percentage compensation leases are outside the protection of the lease exceptions, regardless of whether the lessor is the entity or the referring physician or physician group.

ii. Timeshare Arrangements (§ 411.357(y))

The exception for timeshare arrangements was created through the CY 2016 PFS final rule in order to provide flexibility and protect arrangements that did not involve leasehold interests. In fact, the exception specifically carves out leasehold interests from its protection.[42] The legal relationship of the parties utilizing the exception will essentially be that of licensee/licensor, but CMS declined to include that terminology in the text of the exception out of concern that it might prove to be limiting.[43]

The exception contains many requirements and restrictions.

First, it covers arrangements only between (1) a physician (or a "physician organization" in which shoes the physician stands[44]) and,

---

[42] *See* 42 C.F.R. § 411.357(y)(9).

[43] *See* 80 *Fed. Reg.* at 71328 (middle column).

[44] *See* Chapter 2, section A.5.b.iii. for discussion of the stand-in-the-shoes principle.

(2), a hospital, or a "physician organization" of which the physician in (1) is not an owner, employee, or contractor. The arrangement must be set out in writing, signed by the parties, and specify the premises, equipment, personnel, items, supplies, and services covered by the arrangement.

Second, the compensation under the arrangement is set in advance, consistent with fair market value, commercially reasonable in the absence of referrals between the parties, and not determined in a manner that takes into account the volume or value of referrals or other business generated between the parties. The exception also requires that the compensation not run afoul of certain per-click or percentage-of-revenue restrictions that are similar to those in other exceptions.

Third, space, equipment, personnel, items, supplies, and services covered by the arrangement must be used "predominantly" for the provision of evaluation and management (E&M) services, and "on the same schedule." CMS explains that the latter requirement means that "all locations under the timeshare arrangement, including the premises where E&M services are furnished and the premises where DHS are furnished, must be used on identical schedules."[45]

Fourth, there are restrictions on the type of equipment that may be used under the arrangement and where it may be used and how it may be used. The equipment covered by the arrangement: (1) cannot include advanced imaging equipment, radiation therapy equipment, or clinical or pathology laboratory equipment (other than equipment used to perform CLIA-waived laboratory tests); (2) must be located in the same building where the E&M services are furnished; and (3) cannot be used to furnish DHS other than those incidental to the E&M furnished at the time of the patient's E&M visit.

Fifth, the arrangement may not be conditioned on the referral of patients by the physician party to the arrangement to the hospital or physician organization of which the physician is not an owner, employee, or contractor.

Given all of the requirements and restrictions of this regulatorily created exception, a much better alternative would be the payments by a physician exception, discussed below.

---

[45] *See* 80 Fed. Reg. at 71327 (middle column).

b. *Bona Fide Employment Relationship (411.357(c)); Personal Service Arrangements (§ 411.357(d)(1)) and Fair Market Value Compensation (§ 411.357(l)); Payments by a Physician (§ 411.257(i))*

i. Bona Fide Employment Relationship (§ 411.357(c))

The exception for "bona fide employment relationships" (commonly known as the employee exception) protects referrals from a physician (or immediate family member of the physician) who is an employee of an entity, such as a group practice or hospital. The exception requires that: (1) the employment be for identifiable services; (2) the remuneration paid be consistent with the fair market value of the services; (3) the remuneration would be commercially reasonable even if no referrals were made by the employee to the employer, and (4), effective for referrals made after January 19, 2021, if remuneration to the physician is conditioned on the physician's referrals to a particular provider, practitioner, or supplier, the arrangement satisfies the conditions of § 411.354(d)(4).

Note that the bona fide employment exception does not require the arrangement to be in writing and signed. The lack of a signed writing requirement is unusual, but not unique, with respect to the compensation exceptions. However, it is still recommended, and a best practice, for all employment agreements to be in writing and signed.

Note also that the "volume or value" prohibition is on the direct or indirect taking into account the volume or value of referrals of DHS only—the prohibition does not extend to other business generated. This feature of the employee exception could prove useful. Suppose a physician refers each year, on average, twice as much Medicare DHS as "commercial DHS."[46] It would be improper for the employer to pay a productivity bonus in which the physician would receive 20% of the DHS she referred and 10% of the commercial DHS, but it should be permissible for the employer to pay the physician 30% of the commercial DHS.

---

[46] The term "commercial DHS" is, strictly speaking, a misnomer, just as "Medicare DHS" is redundant, but the terms are used here for the sake of convenience.

The employee exception contains some curious language, which can be explained. The statute provides at section 1877(e)(2)(B)(ii) that the compensation may not be determined in a manner that takes into account (directly or indirectly)[47] the volume or value of referrals for DHS by the referring physician, and then adds language at the end of the exception that subparagraph (B)(ii) does not prohibit a productivity bonus based on services performed personally by the physician. The language at the end of the exception appears unnecessary because subparagraph (B)(ii) does not place any prohibition on compensation for personally performed services but rather the prohibition is on compensation for referrals, and a personally performed service is not a referral.

The explanation is that at the time the statute was drafted there was no rule that said a personally performed service is not a referral (nor was there any rule that a personally performed service was a referral). CMS subsequently excluded a physician's personally performed service from the definition of "referral," but kept the statutory language in the regulatory version of the exception.[48]

ii. Personal Service Arrangements (§ 411.357(d)(1))

The exception for personal service arrangements (also called the PSA exception) complements the bona fide employment exception by protecting arrangements involving independent contractor physicians.[49] Under a typical arrangement between a physician and an entity, the physician would provide certain specified services, such as medical director services or emergency room call. This exception can be used for clinical, administrative, or other types of services.

The exception requires the following elements be met: (1) each arrangement involving the parties is set forth in writing signed by the parties and states the services to be provided; (2) the "arrangement" (actually, the agreement) covers all of the services to be rendered; (3)

---

47 Note that the regulatory exception does not say "directly or indirectly" but uses instead the language "is not determined in any manner." CMS's practice is that unless a regulatory exception specifies that the prohibition is only on the direct taking into account, the prohibition is on both the direct and indirect taking into account.

48 *See* 42 C.F.R. §§ 411.357(c)(2)(ii), (c)(4).

49 42 C.F.R. § 411.357(d).

the aggregate services to be provided do not exceed what is reasonable and necessary for legitimate business purposes; (4) each arrangement lasts for at least one year; (5) the compensation to be paid is set in advance for fair market value without taking into account the volume or value of any referrals or other business generated between the parties; and (6) the services do not involve the counseling or promotion of any activity that violates any federal or state law.

With respect to the second requirement, the regulation adds language beyond the statute, which states that "[t]his requirement [that the "arrangement" covers all the services to be rendered] is met if all separate arrangements between the entity and the physician and the entity and any family members incorporate each other by reference or if they cross-reference a master list of contracts that is maintained and updated centrally and is available for review by the Secretary upon request. The master list must be maintained in a manner that preserves the historical record of contracts." CMS stated in the Phase II final rule that it originally "included the incorporation requirement to fulfill the statutory directive in section 1877(e)(3)(A)(ii) of the Act that arrangements cover all of the services to be provided," and provided an alternative in the Phase II final rule to allow cross-referencing to a master list of contracts that is maintained and updated centrally.[50]

This requirement is a bit silly, and may be the result of poor word choice in the statute. The statute says that, in order to gain the protection of the exception "the arrangement is set out in writing, signed by the parties, and specifies the services covered by the arrangement." But as an intangible, an "arrangement" (as opposed to a writing) cannot specify anything, and therefore CMS's view that there was a statutory "directive" that "arrangements cover all the services provided" is flawed. The statutory sentence should have read: "the arrangement is set out in writing, which is signed by the parties, and specifies the services covered by the arrangement," which is what Congress meant. Congress obviously wanted the written agreement to specify the services that were covered under the compensation set forth in the agreement. There is no reason to think that Congress would object to the parties having multiple agreements, provided

---

[50] *See* 69 Fed. Reg. at 16091.

each one met the requirements of the exception, including specifying the services to be covered under the compensation set forth in the agreement. Tellingly, when promulgating the exception for fair market compensation at section 411.357(l) (which, as a regulatory-created exception must pose no risk of program or patient abuse) CMS expressly decided it was unnecessary to have the incorporation by reference/master list requirement.[51] CMS's persistence in maintaining the incorporation by reference/master list requirement serves little if any purpose and creates a trap for the unwary. For this reason, and others, practitioners should consider structuring arrangements to meet both the PSA exception and the fair market value exception, to the extent possible.

This exception, like the lease exceptions (but unlike the fair market value exception), allows a holdover for an unlimited period, provided that the terms of the underlying arrangement do not change. Of course, to take advantage of a holdover, the arrangement must continue to meet the underlying exception (including continuing to meet the fair market value requirement).

Although in the 2020 final rule CMS retracted its previous statements that office space is neither an item nor service,[52] it reaffirmed its policy that it is not a service, and said that the PSA exception cannot be used to protect arrangements for the rental of office space or time-share arrangements.[53]

iii. Fair Market Value Compensation (§ 411.357(l))

The fair market value exception is another Stark exception with potentially broad application.[54] It is also very similar to the personal service arrangements exception in practice. The exception often

---

[51] *See* 66 Fed. Reg. at 919 ("We agree that it is burdensome to require that the written agreement either cover all items and services to be provided by the physician or immediate family member to the entity, or cross refer to any other agreements for items or services between any of these parties. To alleviate this burden, we are eliminating the requirement that the agreement cross refer to any other agreements.").

[52] *See* 85 Fed. Reg. at 77604, 77624.

[53] *See* 85 Fed. Reg. at 77605.

[54] 42 C.F.R. § 411.357(l).

catches compensation arrangements that do not squarely fit into another exception thereby making such arrangements permissible.

The fair market value exception requires that an arrangement: (1) is in writing, signed by the parties, and specifies the items or services covered; (2) sets the timeframe of the arrangement, provided that the terms do not change within any one-year period; (3) specifies the compensation to be provided, which must be set in advance for fair market value without taking into account the volume or value of referrals or other business generated between the parties; (4) is commercially reasonable and furthers legitimate business purposes; (5) does not violate the Anti-Kickback Statute or any other law or regulation relating to billing or claims submission; and (6) does not promote or counsel any activity that violates any federal or state law. Prior to the 2020 final rule, the exception specifically excluded space rentals from its coverage, requiring such rentals to meet the specific exception for space rentals. In the 2020 final rule, CMS reversed its longstanding position that the provision of rentable space was not an item or service, thereby making office space rentals eligible for protection under the exception.[55]

iv. Payments by a Physician (§ 411.357(i))

The payments by a physician exception took on new importance beginning with the 2019 proposed rule. The exception is a statutory one,[56] which applies to payments from a physician to an entity as compensation for items or services, and requires only that the items or services are furnished at a price consistent with fair market value. There is no requirement for a signed written agreement, no set in advance or commercial reasonableness requirement, and no prohibition on the taking into account the volume or value of referrals. Of course, it would make little sense to construe the exception as applicable when in conflict with another statutory exception, such as the space and equipment lease exceptions (which require a year term and a signed written agreement, among other things). But CMS went further and took the view that if there was another exception potentially applicable to the arrangement, even a regulatory exception

---

55 *See* 85 Fed. Reg. at 77605.

56 Section 1877(e)(8) of the Social Security Act, 42 U.S.C. § 1395nn(e)(8).

(which, by definition, must contain requirements to protect against any risk of program or patient abuse), such as the fair market value compensation exception, the payments by a physician exception was not applicable.[57] In the 2019 proposed rule, CMS essentially confessed error, while maintaining that the exception cannot be relied on to skirt the requirements of a statutory exception that is applicable to the arrangement. The 2020 final rule reiterated the position of the proposed rule and amended the regulatory exception to remove language that said the exception was not applicable to items and services addressed by any other exception, including any regulatory exception. As amended, the regulatory exception provides that it is inapplicable only where a statutory exception is applicable. In other words, CMS no longer takes the position that one cannot use the exception where a regulatory exception, such as the exception for fair market value compensation, would be applicable to the arrangement. To the extent that CMS's restrictive policy toward the statutory payments by a physician exception was ultra vires and recognized as so in the 2019 proposed rule, arguably there is no effective date for the new policy but rather parties should be entitled to rely on the statutory exception as written regardless of the date the arrangement commenced.

Although CMS disavowed its restrictive policy, it also stated that "'items or services' furnished by the entity under the exception for payments by a physician may not include cash or cash equivalents. That is, the physician may not make in-kind 'payments' to the entity in exchange for cash from the entity."[58] It also stated that, whereas the exception cannot be used to protect a lease from an entity for office space, because it retracted its policy that a lease of space is

[57] Note that certain of the statutory exceptions provide the Secretary with the authority to impose additional restrictions, but such authority is lacking with respect to the payments by a physician exception.

[58] *See* 85 Fed. Reg. at 77604. However, CMS also noted that, under its pass-through policy, a physician could pay $10 for a gift card worth $10. This is not because the exception protects such an exchange, but rather where there is an even exchange of cash or cash equivalent, or "where a physician or an entity acts as a pure pass-through, taking money from one party and passing the exact same amount of money to another party, [CMS does] not believe that the pass-through arrangement is a financial relationship for purposes of the physician self-referral law." *See id.* at 77605

neither an item nor a service, the exception can be used to protect payments by a physician for the lease or use of space that is not office space, such as storage space or residential real estate.[59]

c. *Physician Recruitment (§411.357(e)), Physician Retention (§411.357(t)), and Practitioner Recruitment (§ 411.357(x))*

i. Physician Recruitment (§411.357(e))

The "recruitment exception" is an important and often visited exception by those practitioners who have hospitals as clients. It generally allows hospitals[60] to give money (without requiring anything in exchange) to a physician to induce him or her to relocate his or her practice to the hospital's service area and join the hospital's medical staff (but, as true with everything else in Stark, is a bit more involved than that). The exception requires that the recruited physician not be required to refer patients to the hospital and that the amount of remuneration under the recruitment arrangement not be determined in a manner that takes into account (directly or indirectly) the volume or value of any referrals by the referring physician. A written agreement is required for the exception. The recruitment assistance may be passed directly from the hospital to the recruited physician, or the hospital may provide recruitment assistance indirectly to the physician by passing remuneration to a physician practice, which would then be required to pass the remuneration to the physician (while deducting for certain permitted expenses).

Relocation of medical practice and joining the medical staff There are two ways to satisfy the relocation requirement (where the requirement is applicable), and there are certain types of physicians to whom the relocation requirement does not apply.

The first way to satisfy the relocation requirement is for the physician to move his or her medical practice at least 25 miles and *into*

---

[59] *See* 85 Fed. Reg. at 77604.

[60] Federally qualified health centers (FQHCs) and rural health clinics are also covered by the exception to the same extent as hospitals, but rarely enter into physician recruitment arrangements. Therefore, for ease of reference, "hospital" is used throughout this discussion instead of "hospital or FQHC or rural health clinic."

the geographic service area (GSA) of the hospital. The word "into" is important, because it signals that it is not enough for the physician to simply move his or her medical practice, but rather the physician's practice must be located outside of the hospital's geographic service and move *into* the hospital's service area, *and* the distance moved must be at least 25 miles from its original location.

Example 1: Physician's practice is within the GSA of Hospital. Physician moves her practice 30 miles away, which is still within the GSA of Hospital. Relocation requirement is *not* met.

Example 2: Physician lives within the GSA of Hospital but her practice is just outside of the GSA of Hospital. Physician moves her practice 25.5 miles away and into the GSA of Hospital. Relocation requirement is met.

The second way for a physician to satisfy the relocation requirement is to move his medical practice into the GSA of the hospital, without satisfying the 25-miles requirement, while deriving at least 75 percent of his or her practice's revenues from professional services furnished to patients (including hospital inpatients) not seen or treated by the physician at his or her prior medical practice site during the preceding 3 years, measured on an annual basis (fiscal or calendar year). For the initial year of the recruited physician's new practice, the 75-percent test is met if there is a reasonable expectation that the recruited physician's medical practice for the year will derive at least 75 percent of its revenues from professional services furnished to patients not seen or treated by the physician at his or her prior medical practice site during the preceding 3 years.

The relocation requirement does not apply to the following types of physicians:

1. Residents
2. Physicians in practice one year or less
3. Physicians who were employed on a full-time basis for at least two years immediately prior to the recruitment arrangement by one of the following (and who did not maintain a private

practice in addition to such full-time employment): (a) Federal or State bureau of prisons (or similar entity operating one or more correctional facilities) to serve a prison population; (b) Department of Defense or Department of Veterans Affairs to serve active or veteran military personnel and their families; and (c) Indian Health Service facility for serving patients who receive medical care exclusively through the Indian Health Service.

4. Physicians who the Secretary has deemed in an advisory opinion do not have an established medical practice that serves or could serve a significant number of patients who are or could become patients of the recruiting hospital.

Regardless of how the physician satisfies the relocation requirement, or whether the physician is excused from meeting the relocation requirement, the physician must *join* the medical staff of the hospital. The word "join" is important because it signals that the recruited physician cannot already be a member of the recruiting hospital's staff. Moreover, it does not matter if the recruited physician already has some, arguably lesser form of privileges—if the recruited physician has *any* privileges with the recruiting hospital, the recruitment exception cannot be satisfied.[61]

Geographic Service Area (GSA) All recruited physicians—even those who are excused from the relocation requirement—must establish a practice within the recruiting hospital's GSA. The rules on what constitutes the hospital's GSA are somewhat complex.

The general definition for the GSA of a hospital is the area composed of the lowest number of contiguous zip codes from which the hospital draws at least 75 percent of its inpatients. The geographic area served by the hospital may include one or more zip codes from which the hospital draws no inpatients, provided that such zip codes are entirely surrounded by zip codes in the geographic area described above from which the hospital draws at least 75 percent of its inpatients.[62]

---

[61] *See* 72 Fed. Reg. at 51048.
[62] 42 C.F.R. § 411.357(e)(2)(i).

But what about the situation in which a hospital draws fewer than 75 percent of its inpatients from all of the contiguous zip codes from which it draws inpatients? Consider a hospital that has a national or international reputation and accordingly draws patient from across the country or across the globe. For such a hospital, its GSA is area composed of all of the contiguous zip codes from which the hospital draws its inpatients.[63]

There is also a "special optional rule" for rural hospitals. For a hospital located in a rural area, the hospital is permitted to choose, as an alternative test, the area composed of the lowest number of contiguous zip codes from which the hospital draws at least 90 percent of its inpatients. If the hospital draws fewer than 90 percent of its inpatients from all of the contiguous zip codes from which it draws inpatients, the hospital's GSA may include noncontiguous zip codes, beginning with the noncontiguous zip code in which the highest percentage of the hospital's inpatients resides, and continuing to add noncontiguous zip codes in decreasing order of percentage of inpatients.

How much remuneration can the hospital provide? The recruitment exception does not require a fair market value exchange for services. Indeed, CMS has taken the position that a physician furnishes no compensable services under a recruitment arrangement. That said, and although the exception does not specify a dollar limit for the value of remuneration that a hospital may provide under the exception, there are limits nonetheless. The exception protects remuneration from a hospital that is intended to induce a physician to move his or her practice to the hospital's GSA and join the hospital's medical staff, so arguably any remuneration above what it took to induce the physician—or another physician with the same specialty, background, and experience—is not protected. CMS has also issued an advisory opinion in which it held that the exception does not protect additional remuneration given to a physician after a recruitment agreement is finalized.[64]

---

[63] 42 C.F.R. § 411.357(e)(2)(ii)

[64] *See* CMS Advisory Opinion AO-2007-01 (available at https://www.cms.gov/Medicare/Fraud-and-Abuse/PhysicianSelfReferral/Downloads/CMS-AO-2007-01.pdf).

Although theoretically there is a wide variety of types or amounts of remuneration that various hospitals could offer prospective physician recruits, hospitals generally offer income guaranty loans to physicians,[65] coupled with a loan forgiveness feature tied to the physician's presence in the hospital's GSA for some period of time after the recruitment agreement period. The purpose of the income guaranty loan is to make up shortfalls in a recruited physician's collections for professional services. A typical income guaranty loan followed with a forgiveness feature would work as follows:

Hospital extends an income guaranty loan to Physician, which, for two years, will make up any shortfall between what Physician's collections are, after expenses, and $30,000 a month. Together with the recruitment agreement, Physician signs a note for the loan, with a commercially reasonable rate of interest. At the end of the two-year period, Physician must begin paying back any accumulated loan principal plus interest. However, for each month following the end of the recruitment agreement period that Physician continues to practice in Hospital's GSA, Hospital will forgive a certain amount of debt.[66] During the two-year period, Physician occasionally brings in net collections that equal or exceed $30,000, but in most months there is a shortfall that is covered by the income guaranty loan.

CMS recently affirmed the position taken in the advisory opinion in its Explanatory Guidance it issued on the 2020 COVID-19 waivers. There CMS stated:

> We concluded [in CMS-AO-2007-01] that, because the physician would have already relocated his or her medical practice, the additional compensation would not be for the purpose of inducing relocation and may directly or indirectly reflect the volume or value of the recruited physician's actual or potential referrals. . . . CMS-AO-2007-01 remains CMS policy.

See https://www.cms.gov/files/document/explanatory-guidance-march-30-2020-blanket-waivers-section-1877g-social-security-act.pdf.

[65] A typical length of the income guaranty is two or three years.

[66] Some agreements provide that the hospital will forgive one month's worth of debt for each month the physician continues to practice in the hospital's GSA.

Recruited physicians joining a group The exception is a statutory one, and in that form, applies only to recruitment assistance provided by hospitals directly to physicians.[67] In the 2004 Phase II final rule, CMS exercised its statutory authority to expand statutory exceptions or create new exceptions[68] and provided that hospitals may provide recruitment payments that may be made through existing medical groups (rather than directly to the recruited physician).

With respect to remuneration provided by a hospital to a physician either indirectly through payments made to another physician or physician practice, or directly to a physician who joins a physician practice, the exception adds the following requirements:

1. The written recruitment is also signed by the physician practice if the remuneration is provided indirectly to the physician through payments made to the physician practice and the physician practice does not pass directly through to the physician all of the remuneration from the hospital;[69]
2. except for the actual costs incurred by the physician practice in recruiting the new physician, the remuneration is passed directly through to or remains with the recruited physician;
3. in the case of an income guarantee given by the hospital, the costs allocated by the physician practice to the recruited physician do not exceed the actual additional incremental costs attributable to the recruited physician;[70]

[67] *See* section 1877(e)(4) of the Social Security Act, 42 U.S.C. § 1395nn(e)(5).

[68] *See* section 1877(b)(4) of the Social Security Act, 42 U.S.C. § 1395nn(b)(4).

[69] With respect to recruitment arrangements entered into prior to the effective date of the 2020 final rule, the recruitment agreement was required to be signed by the physician practice if the recruitment payments were made directly to the physician practice, irrespective of whether the practice passed all of the remuneration directly to the physician.

[70] There is a special rule for recruited physicians who join a physician practice located in a rural area or HPSA. If the physician is recruited to replace a physician who, within the previous 12-month period, retired, relocated outside of the hospital's GSA, or died, the costs allocated by the physician practice to the recruited physician cannot exceed either (A) The actual additional incremental costs attributable to the recruited physician; or (B) The lower of a per capita allocation or 20 percent of the practice's aggregate costs.

4. records of the actual costs and the passed-through amounts must be maintained for a period of at least six years and made available to the Secretary upon request;
5. the remuneration cannot be determined in any manner that takes into account the volume or value of actual or anticipated referrals by the recruited physician or the physician practice (or any physician affiliated with the physician practice) receiving the direct payments from the hospital; and
6. the physician practice may not impose on the recruited physician practice restrictions that unreasonably restrict the recruited physician's ability to practice medicine in hospital's GSA.

With respect to the last requirement, CMS has stated that a reasonable non-compete is permissible, and that, although a non-compete, or other practice restriction that violates applicable State or local laws is not per se invalid, such a non-compete or other such restriction is suspect.[71] On the other hand, CMS did not say that a non-compete or other restriction that is valid under applicable law is per se reasonable for purposes of the exception.

Note that the IRS has issued guidance for non-profit hospitals that wish to enter into physician recruitment arrangements while not adversely affecting their section 501(c)(3) tax-exempt status.[72]

ii. Physician Retention (§ 411.357(t))

The physician retention exception is the corollary to the physician recruitment exception—it allows a hospital (or rural health clinic or federally qualified health center (FQHC)) to give remuneration to a physician whose practice is in the hospital's GSA to keep his or her practice in the hospital's GSA. The exception applies only to practices in an "underserved area,"[73] and, unlike the physician recruitment

---

[71] *See* 72 Fed. Reg. at 51054 (first column).

[72] *See* Rev. Rul. 97-21, available at https://www.irs.gov/pub/irs-tege/rr1997-21.pdf.

[73] For purposes of the exception, a practice in "underserved area" is one: (1) that is located in a rural area or HPSA; or (2) that is located in an area with demonstrated need for the physician as determined by CMS in an advisory opinion; or (3) for which at least 75 percent of the physician's patients reside in a medically underserved area or are members of a medically underserved population. 42 C.F.R. § 411.357(t)(3).

exception, the remuneration must be paid directly to a physician—it cannot be made to the physician's group.[74]

The exception requires that the physician who is the subject of a retention payment from a hospital (on whose medical staff the physician is a member) must have received a bona fide firm, written recruitment offer or employment offer—or alternatively, where the physician has not yet received a written offer of recruitment or employment, he or she may submit a written certification of a bona fide opportunity of employment from a hospital, academic medical center, or physician organization unrelated to the hospital making the payment, and the offer or opportunity would require the physician to move the location of his or her medical practice at least 25 miles and outside of the GSA of the hospital making the retention payment.[75] More remuneration can be given where there is a bona fide written offer than where the physician relies on a written certification of a bona fide opportunity.

iii. Practitioner Recruitment (§ 411.357(x))

In the 2007 Phase III final rule, CMS noted that a commenter requested that CMS expand the physician recruitment exception to protect remuneration for the recruitment of mid-level non-physician practitioners into a hospital's GSA, including into an existing group practice. CMS responded by saying that it declined to so modify the physician recruitment exception because "[t]hese kinds of subsidy arrangements pose a substantial risk of fraud and abuse."[76] However, in the CY 2016 final rule, CMS said it was comfortable that it had devised an exception that would protect against program and patient abuse while fostering increased access to care.

The exception in some ways parallels the physician recruitment exception and in other ways substantially deviates from that exception. The exception allows a hospital (or FQHC or rural health clinic) to provide remuneration to a physician for the physician to

[74] *See* 73 Fed. Reg. at 51067 (middle column).

[75] *See* 42 C.F.R. § 411.357(t)(1) and (t)(2). The exception specifies requirements for the written offer and for the certification. *See id.*

[76] *See* 73 Fed. Reg. at 51049 (middle and right columns).

compensate a (certain type of) non-physician practitioner[77] (NPP) to provide NPP patient care services.[78] Although the exception speaks of the remuneration from the hospital going to "a physician," the preamble to the final rule makes clear that the required direct compensation arrangement between the hospital and "a physician," includes a physician who stands in the shoes of his or her physician organization. Thus, the qualifying compensation arrangement could be between a hospital and group practice for the purpose of the physician owner of the group practice to provide compensation to an NPP who is an extension of the physician owner's practice.

The exception requires that the arrangement is set forth in writing and signed by the hospital, the physician, and the NPP. The arrangement must commence prior to the compensation arrangement between the physician and the NPP. CMS saw no reason to allow a hospital to provide recruitment assistance for a physician to bring on board an NPP if the NPP was already working for the physician. The exception does not require the NPP to become employed by the physician or the physician organization in whose shoes the physician stands, but rather permits an employment, contractual or "other" arrangement between the physician and the NPP. A qualifying arrangement does not include an ownership or investment interest by the NPP in the physician's physician organization.[79]

The arrangement must not be conditioned on the physician's referrals to the hospital or the NPP's "NPP referrals" to the hospital.[80]

---

77 The types of NPPs eligible for the exception are physician assistant, nurse practitioner, clinical nurse specialist, certified nurse-midwife, clinical social worker, and clinical psychologist. 42 C.F.R. § 411.357(x)(3).

78 "NPP patient care services" is defined as direct patient care services furnished by an NPP that address the medical needs of specific patients or any task performed by an NPP that promotes the care of patients of the physician or physician organization with which the NPP has a compensation arrangement. 42 C.F.R. § 411.357(x)(4)(i).

79 42 C.F.R. § 411.357(x)(6).

80 "NPP referrals" are defined as the request by, or the establishment of a plan of care by, an NPP that includes the provision of DHS, the establishment of any plan of care by an NPP that includes the provision of such a designated health service, or the certifying or recertifying of the need for DHS, but does not include any DHS personally performed by the NPP. 42 C.F.R. § 411.357(x)(4)(ii).

Unlike the physician recruitment exception, there are stated limits on how much remuneration the hospital may provide.

- The remuneration cannot exceed 50 percent of the actual compensation, signing bonus, and benefits paid by the physician to the NPP during a period not to exceed the first two consecutive years of the compensation arrangement between the NPP and the physician (or the physician organization in whose shoes the physician stands).
- The compensation, signing bonus, and benefits paid to the NPP by the physician cannot exceed fair market value for the NPP patient care services furnished by the NPP to patients of the physician's practice.[81]

In addition to allowing only certain types of NPPs to qualify for recruitment assistance, the exception also places restrictions on the NPP's past practice history and the NPP's relationship with the physician (or the physician organization in whose shoes the physician stands).

- The NPP cannot, within one year of the commencement of his or her compensation arrangement with the physician (or the physician organization) have furnished NPP patient care services in the hospital's GSA, or been employed or otherwise engaged to provide NPP patient care services by a physician (or a physician organization) that has a medical practice site located in the hospital's GSA.
- The NPP has a compensation arrangement directly with the physician (or the physician organization in whose shoes the physician stands). The compensation arrangement may be employment, contractual or "other," but an ownership or investment interest in the physician organization is not included.

---

[81] The exception also requires that the remuneration cannot be determined in any manner that takes into account (i) the volume or value of actual or anticipated referrals for DHS or other business generated by the physician (or any physician in the physician's practice), or (ii) NPP referrals by the NPP (or any NPP in the physician's practice) or other business generated between the parties. 42 C.F.R. § 411.357(x)(1)(iii)(B).

- Substantially all of the NPP patient care services that the NPP furnishes to patients of the physician's practice are primary care services or mental health care services.
- The physician cannot impose practice restrictions on the NPP that unreasonably restrict the NPP's ability to provide NPP patient care services in the hospital's GSA.

The exception generally can be relied upon by a hospital only once every 3 years with respect to the same referring physician.[82] However, this limitation does not apply if both of the following requirements are met:

- The NPP is replacing an NPP who terminated his or her employment or contractual arrangement to provide NPP patient care services with the physician (or the physician organization in whose shoes the physician stands) within 1 year of the commencement of the employment or contractual arrangement; and
- The remuneration provided to the physician is provided during a period that does not exceed 2 consecutive years as measured from the commencement of the compensation arrangement between the NPP who is being replaced and the physician (or the physician organization in whose shoes the physician stands).[83]

d. *Indirect Compensation Arrangements (§ 411.357(p))*

The exception for indirect compensation arrangements protects referrals from a physician who has an "indirect compensation arrangement" with an entity.[84] In the past, CMS has stressed that where an indirect compensation arrangement exists, the only *compensation* exception that will protect the arrangement is the exception for indirect compensation arrangements. That is not quite accurate, however. CMS has also acknowledged that the exception for risk-sharing arrangements may be able to protect an indirect compensation arrangement that is created by the risk-sharing arrangement.[85]

[82] 42 C.F.R. § 411.357(x)(7)(i).
[83] 42 C.F.R. § 411.357(x)(7)(ii).
[84] 42 C.F.R. § 411.357(p).
[85] *See* 85 Fed. Reg. at 77525.

Also, a service-based exception, such as the in-office ancillary services exception, may be used to protect referrals of DHS as an indirect compensation arrangement. That is, a service-based exception will not protect the indirect compensation arrangement itself, but may, depending on the circumstances, protect referrals for DHS and other business generated by the physician to the entity with to which the physician has an indirect compensation arrangement.[86] Also, in the 2020 final rule, CMS added a "special rule for indirect compensation arrangements involving value-based arrangements"[87], which recognizes the applicability of the exceptions for value-based arrangements at section 411.357(aa) in certain circumstances. Specifically, the rule provides that, when an unbroken chain of financial relationships includes a "value-based arrangement" which the physician (or the physician organization in whose shoes the physician stands under this paragraph) is a direct party: (1) the DHS entity is not a managed care association (MCO) or an independent practice association (IPA). The only applicable exceptions are the service based exceptions, the exception for indirect compensation arrangements, and the value based exceptions; and (2) the DHS entity is an MCO or IPA. The exception for risk-sharing arrangements[88] is applicable (in addition to the three aforementioned exceptions).[89]

Although the analysis as to whether the *definition* of an "indirect compensation arrangement" is quite complex (see Chapter 2, section A.5.b.iv.), if that analysis is completed and the conclusion is that the definition is met and that the arrangement needs to be protected by the *exception* for indirect compensation arrangements, the analysis of whether the exception is met is mostly straightforward. The exception for indirect compensation arrangements requires that (1) the compensation received by the referring physician from the entity with which the physician has a direct compensation arrangement is fair market value for the services and items actually provided

---

[86] *See* section A.1. of this Chapter 4.

[87] 42 C.F.R. § 411.354(c)(4)(iii).

[88] 42 C.F.R. § 411.357(n).

[89] Note the caveat in the 2020 final rule: "To be clear, the link closest to the physician may not be an ownership interest; it must be a compensation arrangement that meets the definition of value-based arrangement finalized at § 411.351." 85 Fed. Reg. at 77526.

without taking the volume or value of referrals or other business generated into account; (2) the arrangement is set out in writing, signed by the parties,[90] and specifies the services covered; and (3) the arrangement does not violate the Anti-Kickback Statute or any other federal or state law related to billing or claims submission. The exception requires a written agreement between the physician and the entity with which the physician has a direct compensation arrangement, unless the nature of the direct compensation arrangement is an employer–employee relationship.

Prior to the 2020 final rule, many or most indirect compensation arrangements met the exception for indirect compensation arrangements. With the changes made by the 2020 final rule to the aggregate compensation prong of the definition of "indirect compensation arrangement" (which narrows the definition), the opposite is true. In particular, if the reason there is an indirect compensation arrangement is because the compensation from the person or entity with which the referring physician has a direct financial relationship is inconsistent with fair market value, or the physician's unit-based compensation is payment for the lease of equipment or space,[91] the arrangement will necessarily fail the exception. If the reason there is an indirect compensation arrangement is because the amount of compensation the physician receives per individual unit could increase as the number or value of the physician's referrals to (or other business generated for) the entity furnishing DHS increases, or could decrease as the number or value of the physician's referrals to (or other business generated for) the entity decreases,[92] the analysis of whether the exception is failed is more nuanced.

e. *Isolated Transactions (§ 411.357(f))*

The isolated transactions exception can play a large role in the sale of a medical practice or other one-time transactions.[93] A transaction satisfies the exception if: (1) the remuneration under the transaction

---

[90] A written agreement is not required if the physician is an employee of the entity with which he or she has a direct compensation arrangement.

[91] *See* 42 C.F.R. § 411.354(c)(2)(ii)(A)(2)(i) and (iv).

[92] *See* 42 C.F.R. § 411.354(c)(2)(ii)(A)(2)(ii) and (iii).

[93] 42 C.F.R. § 411.357(f). "Transaction" is defined as an instance or process of two or more persons or entities doing business. 42 C.F.R. § 411.351 (Transaction).

is for fair market value without taking into account the volume or value of referrals or other business generated between the parties; (2) the remuneration is commercially reasonable even if no referrals were made; and (3) the parties do not engage in any other transactions for six months, except for transactions that meet a Stark exception or commercially reasonable post-closing adjustments.

An isolated financial transaction can involve either a single payment or installment payments. If installment payments are used, the following elements must be present: (1) the total aggregate payment is set prior to the first payment being made and does not take into account, directly or indirectly, the volume or value of referrals or other business generated by the referring physician; and (2) the payments are immediately negotiable or are guaranteed by a third party, or secured by a negotiable promissory note, or subject to a similar mechanism.[94]

In the commentary to the 2020 final rule CMS took pains to distinguish between installment payments made in connection with a single transaction and multiple payments for multiple services—the latter cannot be protected under the exception for isolated transactions.[95] Examples of multiple payments for multiple services include an employment arrangement or PSA between a hospital and the physician following the sale of the physician's practice to the hospital.

Over the years, some have contended (incorrectly in the author's view) that the exception could cure—and do so retroactively—a noncompliant arrangement through one party making a one-time payment to the other. For example, suppose a physician enters into a PSA with an entity and begins performing services, but the parties cannot agree on the rate of compensation and therefore do not enter into a signed, written agreement. If the parties reach agreement on the compensation some time thereafter and enter into a signed written agreement, some believed that the entity could make a lump-sum payment to the physician for the period prior to the parties signing an agreement and protect the payment under the isolated transaction exception. The 2020 final rule firmly rejects this idea.[96] CMS added

[94] 42 C.F.R. § 411.351 (isolated transaction).

[95] *See* 85 Fed. Reg. at 77576.

[96] *See* 85 Fed. Reg. at 77576-77 ("We remind parties that the provision of remuneration in the form of services commences a compensation arrangement at the

new paragraph (4) to the regulation text to clarify that the settlement of a bona fide legal dispute is a separate compensation arrangement from any compensation arrangement between the parties giving rise to the bona fide dispute, and settlement of a bona fide dispute, though protectable under the exception for isolated transactions,[97] does not retroactively bring the compensation arrangement that gave rise to the dispute into compliance.[98]

f. Remuneration Unrelated to the Provision of DHS (§411.357(g))

The statutory name for this exception is given above, but the regulatory name is "certain arrangements with hospitals." The statutory exception is brief and simply says that a compensation arrangement does not include "remuneration which [sic] is provided by a hospital to a physician if such remuneration does not relate to the provision of designated health services." The legislative history gives no clue as to what the drafter(s) meant by "does not relate to the provision of designated health services." CMS, understandably concerned that if the exception were construed broadly (or, one might say, taken literally) could render the statute largely ineffective with respect to compensation arrangements between hospitals and referring physicians, considerably expanded the requirements of the exception through the regulatory exception.[99]

Under the regulatory version of the exception, the remuneration must be wholly unrelated, directly or indirectly, to the furnishing

---

time the services are provided, and the compensation arrangement must satisfy the requirements of an applicable exception *at that time* if the physician makes referrals for designated health services and the entity wishes to bill Medicare for such services. Thus, the exception for isolated transactions is not available to retroactively cure noncompliance with the physician self-referral law.") (emphasis in the original).

97 CMS reiterated its longstanding policy that the exception can be used to settle a bona fide dispute between the parties, and made changes to the definition of "isolated transaction" at section 411.351 and to the chapeau of the text of the exception for isolated transactions to make this position clear. *See* 85 Fed. Reg. at 77577.

98 *See id.*

99 Note that this is not one of the statutory exceptions for which Congress gave the Secretary the authority to add conditions to the exception to protect against fraud and abuse.

of DHS. The regulatory exception then states that remuneration is related to DHS if it:

1. Is an item, service, or cost that could be allocated in whole or in part to Medicare or Medicaid under cost-reporting principles;
2. Is furnished, directly or indirectly, explicitly or implicitly, in a selective, targeted, preferential, or conditioned manner to medical staff or other persons in a position to make or influence referrals; or
3. Otherwise takes into account the volume or value of referrals or other business generated by the referring physician.[100]

The 2019 proposed rule would have significantly expanded the reach of the exception. The 2019 proposed rule would have provided that remuneration is not related to DHS if it is not determined in any manner that takes into account the volume or value of the physician's referrals, and the remuneration is for an item or service that is not related to the provision of patient care services. The proposed rule then offered a broad definition of patient care services for purposes of the exception, including a proposed deeming that a service would be not related to the provision of patient care services if the service could be provided by a person who is not a licensed medical professional.

The 2020 final rule did not adopt the proposed revised exception, citing, among other things, that the proposed revision could risk program or patient abuse. However, in the 2020 final rule CMS effectively admitted that the current exception is inconsistent with the statute because it is practically meaningless, and that the proposed revision was intended "[t]o give appropriate meaning to the statutory exception."[101]

Unless and until the exception is revised, parties who structure an arrangement to meet the exception (and only the exception) do so at their peril. However, parties should keep the exception in mind when faced with the situation in which they must either find an exception to protect an executed arrangement or do a self-disclosure or

---

[100] 42 C.F.R. § 411.357(g)(1) – (3).

[101] *See* 85 Fed. Reg. at 77601 (third column).

where they must defend against an FCA action. If they can fit the arrangement within the exception as presently constituted, so much the better, but if not, the regulation may be susceptible to challenge as arbitrary and capricious. In particular, the regulatory exception references Medicaid and other business generated, which, by definition, do not relate to DHS. Also, the decision in Phase II to reverse course on the 1998 proposed rule's determination that remuneration for administrative services is unrelated to DHS appears to be a mistake that CMS has now acknowledged by its shift in focus to patient care services.

g. Nonmonetary Compensation (§ 411.357(k))

The exception for nonmonetary compensation allows an entity to provide a physician up to $300 in a calendar year, plus an adjustment for inflation, in nonmonetary compensation.[102] "Nonmonetary" excludes cash and cash equivalents (such as a gift card). Nonmonetary compensation cannot be determined in any manner that takes into account the volume or value of referrals or other business generated by the referring physician, and it cannot be solicited by the physician or the physician's practice (including employees and staff members). The exception also allows an entity that has a formal medical staff to provide one local medical staff appreciation event per year for the entire medical staff without having the value of staff appreciation event count toward the annual limit; however, any gifts or gratuities provided in connection with the event are subject to annual limit.

The exception provides a safety valve for entities that inadvertently exceed the annual limit, with some restrictions. Specifically, such excess compensation must not be more than 50 percent of the limit, and the physician must return to the entity the excess nonmonetary compensation (or an amount equal to the value of the excess nonmonetary compensation) by the end of the calendar year in which

---

[102] The 2023 annual limit was $489.00. The annual limit is published by CMS on its Physician Self-Referral webpage. *See* https://www.cms.gov/medicare/fraud-and-abuse/physicianselfreferral/cpi-u_updates. CMS states that an entity may not use the exception to provide non-monetary compensation to a physician group. *See* 66 Fed. Reg. at 921 (third column) ("The exception for non-monetary compensation up to $300 only protects gifts to individual physicians"); *see also* 69 Fed. Reg. at 16112 (middle column).

the excess nonmonetary compensation was received or within 180 consecutive calendar days following the date the excess nonmonetary compensation was received by the physician, whichever is earlier. Finally, an entity may take advantage of this provision only once every 3 years with respect to the same referring physician.

h. Medical Staff Incidental Benefits (§ 411.357(m))

The medical staff incidental benefits exception bears some similarity to the nonmonetary compensation exception. It allows hospitals and other entities that have formal medical staffs to provide nonmonetary compensation up to a limit of $25 per occurrence of the benefit (e.g., each meal during a day) plus an adjustment for inflation.[103] The prototypical (but far from the sole) example of such compensation is free cafeteria meals to medical staff members. The exception requires that the compensation is offered to all members of the medical staff practicing in the same specialty (but not necessarily accepted by every member to whom it is offered) and that it not be offered in any manner that takes into account the volume or value of referrals or other business generated between the parties. The compensation must be reasonably related to the provision of, or designed to facilitate directly or indirectly the delivery of, medical services at the entity.

Except with respect to identification of medical staff on the entity's website or the entity's advertising, the compensation is provided only during periods when the medical staff members are making rounds or are engaged in other services or activities that benefit the entity or its patients. The compensation must be provided by the entity, and used by the members on campus.[104] CMS has acknowledged that some benefits that are covered by this exception may also be covered by

[103] The 2023 limit is less than $42.00 with respect to each occurrence of the benefit (for example, each meal given to a physician while he or she is serving patients.) The annual limit is published by CMS on its Physician Self-Referral webpage. See https://www.cms.gov/medicare/fraud-and-abuse/physicianselfreferral/cpi-u_updates.

[104] Compensation, including, but not limited to, internet access, pagers, or two-way radios, used away from the campus only to access hospital medical records or information or to access patients or personnel who are on the hospital campus, as well as the identification of the medical staff on a hospital website or in hospital advertising, meets the "on campus" requirement.

an employment arrangement;[105] thus, provided that such benefits do not throw the employment arrangement out of fair market value, the employee exception could be used to protect certain benefits while preserving the per occurrence limit under the medical staff incidental benefits exception for other benefits.

i. Risk-Sharing Arrangements (§ 411.357(n))

This exception protects compensation paid directly or indirectly by a managed care organization (MCO) or an independent practice association (IPA) to a physician pursuant to a risk-sharing arrangement (including, but not limited to, withholds, bonuses, and risk pools) for services provided by the physician to enrollees of a health plan.[106] The exception applies to payments made directly or through a subcontractor, and is applicable to all qualifying risk-sharing arrangements with a physician (regardless of whether the physician is in solo practice, part of a group, works for an academic medical center, and regardless of whether the physician is employed or is an independent contractor).

In Phase II, CMS clarified that the exception is meant to cover all risk-sharing compensation paid to physicians by an entity downstream of any type of health plan, insurance company, HMO, or IPA, provided that the arrangement relates to enrollees and meets the conditions set forth in the exception, and that all downstream entities, including hospitals, are included. Some practitioners read the Phase II commentary (or perhaps the text of the exception itself) to mean that compensation from a hospital to a physician could be protected under the risk-sharing exception, provided that the hospital and the concomitant compensation were part of the risk-sharing arrangement. In the 2020 final rule, however, CMS stated that "[t]he exception

---

[105] *See* 66 Fed. Reg. at 920. CMS added the qualifier "provided [the benefits] are specified in the employment agreement." *Id.* This is incorrect. The parties may have the burden to show that the employment arrangement included the benefits in question, but the employee exception does not require a written agreement in the first place.

[106] The exception defines "health plan" and "enrollees" by reference to the definitions of those terms in the Anti-Kickback Statute safe harbor at 42 C.F.R. § 1001.952(l) for increased coverage, reduced cost-sharing amounts, or reduced premium amounts offered by health plans. CMS purposefully declined to define "managed care organization" "so as to create a broad exception with more maximum flexibility." *See* 66 Fed. Reg. at 16114.

does not apply to a compensation arrangement—whether direct or indirect—between a physician and an entity that is anything other than an MCO or IPA."[107] CMS acknowledged the potential confusion the Phase II commentary referred to above may have caused, but said it was clarifying that the exception protects compensation only from an MCO or IPA. Accordingly, the pre-2020 final rule language at the beginning of the exception, "[c]ompensation pursuant to a risk-sharing arrangement . . . " has now been replaced by "[c]ompensation paid directly or indirectly by a MCO or an IPA to a physician pursuant to a risk-sharing arrangement . . . ."[108]

The upshot of the "clarification" in the 2020 final rule, is that, although CMS continues to describe the risk-sharing arrangement as broad,[109] it appears that instead it has very limited utility. Neither an MCO nor an IPA bills Medicare FFS in the normal course of business and thus neither is an "entity" in the first place.

j. Limited Remuneration to a Physician (§ 411.357(z))

In the 2020 final rule, CMS created a new exception to address situations in which remuneration was provided to a physician in the absence of a signed, written agreement. There is an annual aggregate limit of $5000 (adjusted for inflation) that an entity may provide per physician (and the entity is not limited as to the number of physicians for which it can provide remuneration up to the limit). The compensation may not be determined in any manner that takes into account the volume or value of referrals or other business generated by the physician, it must not exceed fair market value, and the arrangement must be commercially reasonable even if no referrals were made between the parties. By not requiring a signed, written agreement the exception is designed to reduce the need for and the number of Self-Referral Disclosure Protocol (SRDP) disclosures.

Note that compensation from an entity to a physician for items or services provided outside of the arrangement to be protected by the

---

107 *See* 85 Fed. Reg. at 77514.

108 *See* 85 Fed. Reg. at 77528, 77675.

109 *See* 85 Fed. Reg. at 77512 ("as we noted in Phase II, [the risk-sharing arrangement] is intended to be a broad exception with maximum flexibility").

limited remuneration to a physician exception will not count toward the $5000 limit if such items or services provided are protected under a service-based exception or a compensation exception.[110] If the entity has multiple undocumented, unsigned arrangements with the physician, CMS considers the parties to have a single compensation arrangement for the various items and services furnished under such arrangements, and the aggregate compensation provided under such arrangements may not exceed the annual $5000 limit (as adjusted) if they are to be protected under the limited remuneration to a physician exception.[111]

The exception permits the physician to furnish items or services through: employees whom the physician has hired for the purpose of performing the services; through a wholly-owned entity; or through locum tenens physicians (as defined at section 411.351, except that the physician who is being temporarily replaced by the locum tenens physician does not have to be a "member" of a "group practice").[112] Because CMS has reversed its previous stance that office space is neither an item or a service, the exception may be applicable to the lease of space.[113]

There are additional restrictions in the case of space or equipment that is furnished by the physician. The exception requires that

---

> Compensation for the lease of office space or equipment is not determined using a formula based on
>
> 1. A percentage of the revenue raised, earned, billed, collected, or otherwise attributable to the services performed or business generated in the office space or to the services performed on or business generated through the use of the equipment; or

---

[110] *See* 85 Fed. Reg. at 77624 (middle column). CMS continues to maintain that office space is not a service. *See* 85 Fed. Reg. at 77605 (middle column).

[111] *See* 85 Fed. Reg. at 77624.

[112] 42 C.F.R. § 411.357(z)(2).

[113] *See 85* Fed. Reg. at 77624 (middle column).

2. Per-unit-of-service rental charges, to the extent that such charges reflect services provided to patients referred by the lessor to the lessee.[114]

The use of "lease of office space or equipment" in the opening line and "rental charges" and "lessor to the lessee" indicates that the restrictions apply only where there is a leasehold interest involved. The following language in the preamble, however, suggests that the restrictions apply *only* to *timeshare arrangements*, which, by definition, exclude a leasehold interest:[115] "Lastly, we are modifying the [2019 proposed rule's] per-click and percentage-based compensation provisions at § 411.357(z)(1)(v), to clarify that these provisions only apply to timeshare arrangements for the use of premises or equipment."[116] Further adding to the confusion is preamble language that suggests that the restrictions apply to *both* leases and timeshare arrangements: "the exception at § 411.357(z) incorporates prohibitions on percentage-based and per-unit-of-service compensation to the extent the remuneration is for *the use or lease* of office space or equipment, similar to the provisions at existing § 411.357(p)(1)(ii) for indirect compensation arrangements and § 411.357(y)(6)(ii) for timeshare arrangements."[117]

Interestingly, not only is there no set in-advance requirement in this exception, but commentary in the 2020 final rule indicates that the exception for limited remuneration to a physician exception can be used to protect remuneration that an entity provides to a physician as a modification to an arrangement that was protected by an exception that *does* have a set in-advance requirement. To explain, suppose Physician and Hospital have a personal services arrangement, under which compensation was set at $100 per hour. The arrangement is protected by the exception for personal service arrangements or the fair market value compensation exception. Both of those exceptions

---

114 *See* 42 C.F.R. § 411.357(z)(1)(v).

115 *See* 42 C.F.R. § 411.357(y)(9) ("[t]he [timeshare] arrangement does not convey a possessory leasehold interest in the office space that is the subject of the arrangement").

116 *See* 85 Fed. Reg. at 77624 (left column).

117 *See id.* at 77624 (middle column) (emphasis added)

require that compensation be set in advance, and elsewhere in the 2020 final rule CMS makes clear that modifications to the compensation terms of such an arrangement must be made prospectively (i.e., before the delivery of items or services),[118] and that the 90-day grace period for signatures and writings does not absolve one from meeting the set-in-advance requirement.[119] Yet the 2020 final rule commentary states that a modification to compensation may be made prior to, or even without, any signed amendment and such modified compensation can be protected by the exception for limited remuneration to a physician if the amount of additional compensation is less than $5000 and the exception's requirements are otherwise met.[120] Thus, under the example above, on November 15, the parties could amend the PSA so that compensation is $150 per hour November 1. The amended compensation could be protected by the exception for limited remuneration to a physician, provided that the excess compensation (the additional $50 per hour) would not exceed $5000 by the end of the calendar year and the other requirements of the exception for limited remuneration (including fair market value) are met.

k. *EHR and Cybersecurity Exceptions (§ 411.357(w) and § 411.357(bb))*

The exception for electronic health records items and services (EHR exception) allows an entity to provide nonmonetary remuneration (consisting of items and services in the form of software or information technology and training services, including cybersecurity software and services) necessary and used predominantly to create, maintain, transmit, receive, or protect electronic health records. The inclusion of cybersecurity software and services was added by the 2020 final rule. The provision of hardware is not protected. The items and services may be provided by any entity, except for a laboratory. Software must be "interoperable," as defined in section § 411.351, at the time it is provided to the physician. Software is *deemed* to be

---

118 *See id.* at 77591-92.

119 *See id.* at 77579 (third column), 77580 (first column). *See also* 42 C.F.R. § 411.354(d)(1)(C).

120 *See* 85 Fed. Reg. at 77582. Ironically, if the compensation to a physician was reduced without a prospective modification signed by the parties, there would be no exception to protect the modified compensation.

interoperable if, on the date it is provided to the physician, it is certified by a certifying body authorized by the National Coordinator for Health Information Technology. The exception requires that the physician must pay at least 15 percent of the entity's cost for the items and services, and importantly, must make that payment prior to receipt of the items and services.[121]

Other conditions include: neither the physician nor the physician's practice (including employees and staff members) makes the receipt of items or services, or the amount or nature of the items or services, a condition of doing business with the donor; and, neither the eligibility of a physician for the items or services, nor the amount or nature of the items or services, is determined in any manner that *directly* takes into account the volume or value of referrals or other business generated between the parties.[122]

The 2020 final rule removed the sunset provision for the exception, making the exception permanent.[123]

In addition to including cybersecurity technology among the protected items and services for purposes of the EHR exception, the 2020 final rule also established a standalone exception for the provision of nonmonetary remuneration consisting of technology and services necessary and used predominantly to implement, maintain, or reestablish cybersecurity (cybersecurity exception).[124]

The cybersecurity exception is similar to the EHR exception, but it does not have a cost-sharing requirement; it allows donations of hardware,[125] and it does not disqualify labs from providing donations

---

[121] With respect to items and services received after the initial provision of items and services (including replacement items and services), the physician must pay at least 15 percent of the entity's cost for the items and services at reasonable intervals.

[122] The regulations text set forth examples in which the provision of the items or services will be deemed not to take into account directly the volume or value of referrals. However, *see* section B.3. of Chapter 2 for a discussion on the potential problems caused by the new (2020) definition of taking into account the volume or value of referrals on indirect takings into account.

[123] *See* 85 Fed. Reg. at 77613-14.

[124] 42 C.F.R. § 411.357(bb).

[125] In the 2020 final rule CMS stated that it was "modifying the [proposed] definition of 'technology' [at § 411.357(bb)(2)] to remove the phrase 'other than hardware.' Thus, the cybersecurity exception is applicable to hardware that is necessary and used predominantly to implement, maintain, or reestablish cybersecurity." *See* 85 Fed. Reg. at 77639.

of cybersecurity technology. One practical difference between the two exceptions is that if the entity wishes to protect the provision of both EHR items and services and cybersecurity software or services, the physician recipient must contribute 15 percent of the donor's cost for the cybersecurity software or services (as well as the EHR items and services). Like the EHR exception, there is a prohibition on only directly taking into account the volume or value of referrals or other business generated when making the provision of the cybersecurity technology, but there is no list of examples in which the provision would be deemed to satisfy this requirement. CMS explained that it was concerned that a deeming provision could cause parties to forego legitimate and acceptable selection criteria, thus limiting the scope and utility of the exception.[126]

l. Value-Based Arrangement Exceptions (§ 411.357(aa)(1) – (3))

In the 2020 final rule, CMS finalized three exceptions for value-based arrangements, one for arrangements in which the parties bear full financial risk, one for arrangements in which the physician(s) bear meaningful downside financial risk, and one for arrangements in which the parties do not bear financial risk.[127] The exceptions are complex, and are accompanied by definitions that practitioners need to understand before advising clients on the exceptions.[128] A thorough reading of the preamble discussion of the exceptions in the 2019 and 2020 proposed and final rule is highly recommended before advising on the exceptions.

The three exceptions are similar to (but not the same as) the three AKS safe harbors for value-based arrangements that were promulgated by the OIG in its 2020 final rule. Of particular note is the basic

---

126 *See* 85 Fed. Reg. at 77641. *See* section B.3. of Chapter 2 for a discussion on the potential problems caused by the new (2020) definition of taking into account the volume or value of referrals on indirect takings into account.

127 42 C.F.R. § 411.357(aa)(1), (aa)(2) and (aa)(3). The OIG's 2020 final rule promulgated three safe harbors that are similar to the three Stark exceptions. *See* 42 C.F.R. §§ 1001.952 (gg), (ff) and (ee).

128 *See* 42 C.F.R. § 411.351 for definitions of target patient population, value-based activity, value-based arrangement, value-based enterprise, value-based purpose, and value-based enterprise participant.

construct that the exception (and corresponding safe harbor) that requires the most risk has the least amount of requirements.

m. Other Remaining Compensation Exceptions

The following are other exceptions of which practitioners should be aware that are straightforward in their approach or are of little or no use: group practice arrangements with a hospital (§ 411.357(h)); charitable donations by a physician (§ 411.357(j)); compliance training (§ 411.357(o)); referral services (§ 411.357(q)); obstetrical malpractice insurance subsidies (§ 411.357(r)); professional courtesy (§ 411.357(s)); community-wide health systems (§ 411.357(u)); and electronic prescribing items and services (§ 411.357(v)).

n. The Section 353 Exceptions and Special Rule for Reconciling Compensation

Section 411.353 contains two exceptions to the Stark Law prohibition on payment for compensation arrangements that do not meet a compensation exception or a service-based exception. They are mentioned here not because they are particularly useful—indeed they will rarely apply. But because they are so narrow in their application and because they do not appear amongst the "real" exceptions in sections 411.355-357, they are not often given much thought. Given the strict liability nature of Stark, one should always keep in mind, if only in the back of the mind, any potential safety valve.

The first exception allows payment to be made to an entity that submits a claim for DHS if the entity did not have actual knowledge of, and did not act in reckless disregard or deliberate ignorance of, the identity of the physician who made the referral for the DHS at issue.[129] In the great majority of the cases, the DHS entity will have actual knowledge of the identity of the referring physician. The Phase II final rule gave examples of the applicability of the provision:

> for example, when a physician has caused a referral to be made by someone else or has directed or routed a referral through an

---

[129] 42 C.F.R. § 411.353(e). The exception also requires that the claim otherwise complies with all applicable Federal and State laws, rules, and regulations.

intermediary) or are oral referrals (that is, no written request or other documentation that would identify the referring physician is required).[130]

It is important to know that the exception requires that the entity not know or act in reckless disregard of the physician's *identity*. It is not sufficient that the entity not know or act in reckless disregard that the physician (or immediate family member) has a financial relationship with it (or that the financial relationship is not excepted).[131]

The second exception, for "certain arrangements involving temporary noncompliance," provides that payment may be made to an entity for an otherwise prohibited referral if the financial relationship between the entity and the referring physician fully complied with an applicable exception under § 411.355, 411.356, or 411.357 for at least 180 consecutive calendar days immediately preceding the date on which the financial relationship became noncompliant with the exception, and the financial relationship fell out of compliance with the exception for reasons beyond the control of the entity, and the entity promptly takes steps to rectify the noncompliance. ("Promptly" means no more than 90 consecutive calendar days following the date on which the financial relationship became noncompliant with an exception.) The exception may be used by an entity only once every three years with respect to the same referring physician, and the exception does not apply if the exception with which the financial relationship previously complied was the exception for nonmonetary compensation (§ 411.357(k)) or medical staff benefits (§ 411.357(m)).[132]

---

130 69 Fed. Reg. at 16063.

131 In the Phase II final rule CMS rejected a commenter's suggestion that the provision could be used in the situation in which the DHS entity does not have actual knowledge that the referring physician has an immediate family with a financial relationship with the DHS entity, saying that "[t]he statute clearly contemplates a strict liability bar on direct financial relationships with immediate family members. The exception proposed by the commenter would effectively negate the statutory prohibition." *Id.* at 16064.

132 42 C.F.R. § 411.353(f).

There is preamble discussion in the Phase II final rule concerning the exception that indicates that the purpose of the exception was to address such situations as a change in rural status that affects an entity's compliance with the rural provider exception, or the removal of a HPSA designation in an area.[133] Interestingly, the preamble suggests that delays in obtaining fully-signed copies of renewal agreements could fit under the exception,[134] but the circumstances in which an entity's inability to procure a signed renewal agreement is beyond the control of the entity would not seem to include the entity's inability to persuade the physician to sign the agreement on the same terms as the expiring agreement. That CMS provided for an unlimited holdover period for certain exceptions in the CY 2016 PFS final rule provides some relief for the situation in which a physician refuses to sign an extension to an expiring agreement while the parties continue to negotiate.

There is a special rule for reconciling compensation, at section 411.353(h), which is discussed in Chapter 2 as part of the discussion of the period of disallowance.

4. Waivers

a. Section 1135 Waivers

Section 1135 of the Social Security Act gives the Secretary the authority waive certain specific requirements related to Medicare, including "sanctions under section 1877(g) (relating to limitations on physician referral)." [135]

In order to trigger the section 1135 authority, there must be both (1) a public health emergency declared by the Secretary pursuant to section 319 of the Public Health Service Act, and (2) an emergency or disaster declared by the President pursuant to the National Emergencies Act or the Robert T. Stafford Disaster Relief and Emergency Assistance Act.[136] The waivers, which typically would not be issued immediately after the public health emergency/national emergency

---

133 *See* 69 Fed. Reg. at 16057.

134 *Id.*

135 Section 1135(b)(4) of the Social Security Act, 42 U.S.C. § 1320b–5(b)(4).

136 Section 1135(a), (g)(1) of the Social Security Act, 42 U.S.C. 1320b–5(b)(4)(a), (g)(1).

or disaster, may be given retroactive effect.[137] Immediately upon a declaration that the public health emergency *or* the national emergency or disaster has ceased, any waivers disappear.[138]

In response to the COVID-19 pandemic, CMS issued "blanket" Stark waivers on March 30, 2020, which were made retroactive to March 1, 2020. The waivers are referred to as "blanket" waivers, because they apply nationwide and according to their terms, and without regard to individual circumstances. CMS also stated that individual or case-by-case waivers were available upon request. CMS issued 18 blanket waivers. In order to qualify for any of the waivers, however, "the remuneration and referrals described in the blanket waivers must be solely related to COVID-19 Purposes."[139] CMS followed up its issuance of the blanket waivers with Explanatory Guidance that was posted less than a month later.[140]

b. Section 1115A Waivers

Section 1115A(a)(1) of the Social Security Act[141] created the Center for Medicare and Medicaid Innovation (CMMI) within CMS for the purpose of testing innovative payment and service delivery models to reduce program expenditures while preserving or enhancing the quality of care. In furtherance of that purpose, Section 1115A(d)(l)[142] of the Act authorizes the Secretary to waive requirements of title XVIII of the Social Security Act (along with requirements of title XI and certain specified sections of title XIX). Accordingly, CMS has issued waivers of Stark for many of the CMMI models. Unlike the Section 1135 blanket waivers discussed above, the CMMI model waivers do not pertain to certain requirements of the exceptions for certain types of arrangements, but rather typically declare that Stark does not apply to distributions of shared savings or gainsharing or other types or payments. CMS maintains a listing

---

137 Section 1135(c) of the Social Security Act, 42 U.S.C. § 1320b–5(c).

138 Section 1135(e) of the Social Security Act, 42 U.S.C. § 1320b–5(e).

139 *See* https://www.cms.gov/files/document/covid-19-blanket-waivers-section-1877g.pdf.

140 *See* https://www.cms.gov/files/document/explanatory-guidance-march-30-2020-blanket-waivers-section-1877g-social-security-act.pdf.

141 42 U.S.C. § 1315a(a)(1).

142 42 U.S.C. § 1315a(d)(1).

of the CMMI model waivers on its website.[143] The waivers must be read with care because they apply only according to the terms that are set forth.

Accordingly, practitioners who have clients involved in a CMMI payment model should evaluate whether a Stark waiver would be helpful and whether one exists.

---

143 *See* https://www.cms.gov/Medicare/Fraud-and-Abuse/PhysicianSelfReferral/Downloads/CEC-LDO-Model-Waivers.pdf.

5
Interpretations of the Stark Law

OUTLINE

The Stark Law is difficult both to understand and to comply with in the real world.

The complexity of Stark is aggravated by the paucity of available interpretations. CMS has produced guidance and interpretations over time, but the material from CMS can be conflicting as CMS's views evolve and change. Few courts have tackled Stark and its many regulations. The handful of courts that have reviewed the Stark Law have produced written decisions of uncertain value, with some of the decisions giving less than fully accurate renditions of the law and the regulations.

The available guidance falls into three categories: (1) commentary in the Federal Register in connection with the various rulemakings; (2) CMS advisory opinions and frequently asked questions; and (3) case law. Each of these sources provides insight into how the Stark Law and the Stark Regulations are applied or viewed by CMS, other governmental agencies, and the courts. The various sources also present traps for the unwary due to, for example, changes in interpretation over time or incorrect statements in the available case law.[1]

A. Regulatory Preambles and Commentary in the Federal Register

The Federal Register publications of the various proposed and final Stark rules contain the most comprehensive and authoritative interpretation of the regulations. With respect to certain exceptions, it is possible to see where CMS retreated on a restrictive approach or conversely took away a previously broad interpretation of the law. When analyzing a Stark issue, it is both necessary and informative to review the changes to a particular exception in order to understand how an arrangement or relationship may be structured to comply with the law.

The proposed rules contain an explanation from CMS for the purpose of a proposed change. The explanation provides a justification and basis for the change, which then invites comments from interested parties. Comments may influence how a rule is actually finalized. The final rules then contain synopses of certain (but not necessarily all) comments and CMS's responses thereto. In the responses, CMS usually states whether and why it agrees or disagrees with a comment. Accordingly, the comment and response dialogue in the Federal Register is often a very useful tool when performing a Stark analysis (but one must take care that one is considering all of the comment and response dialogue on the issue at hand, including the latest dialogue).

---

[1] In the past, CMS would issue informal guidance through email responses to practitioners who raised specific questions, but that practice has been largely curtailed or eliminated in recent years.

B. CMS Advisory Opinions and FAQs

The Stark Law and the Stark Regulations require that CMS issue written advisory opinions upon request and submission by an interested party.[2] The regulations contain detailed information on the process for requesting an advisory opinion, including the information that must be included in a request, the fees for obtaining an opinion, and a certification statement.[3] Note that CMS does not issue advisory opinions on hypothetical situations—the request must relate to an existing arrangement or a proposed arrangement that, if the opinion is favorable, the requestor, in good faith, plans to enter.[4] CMS will not address in an advisory opinion whether remuneration under the actual or proposed arrangement is consistent with fair market value, or whether an individual is a bona fide employee within the meaning of the Internal Revenue Code.[5]

CMS has issued relatively few advisory opinions related to the Stark Law, and the length of time between the request of the opinion and its issuance is typically more than a year, but the few opinions available may still provide useful guidance in specific factual scenarios. Although an opinion is binding on CMS only with respect to the requestor and as to the specific factual situations presented in the request,[6] the opinions nevertheless provide useful insights into how CMS will apply the legal standards of the Stark Law and which types of factual scenarios may be viewed as complying or not complying with an exception or as outside of Stark altogether.[7] Although an advisory opinion cannot be legally relied upon by a third party, as a practical matter, it would be unusual for CMS to take a position that is inconsistent with the position it took in an advisory opinion unless it has signaled in advance that it has changed its view, or unless the applicable law or regulations have been changed. And in the absence of some communicated change in CMS's position and/or change in

---

[2] 42 U.S.C. § 1395nn(g)(6).

[3] 42 C.F.R. §§ 411.370–411.389.

[4] 42 C.F.R. § 411.370(b)(1).

[5] 42 C.F.R. § 411.370(c).

[6] 42 C.F.R. § 411.387.

[7] Advisory opinions issued by CMS can be accessed at: http://www.cms.gov/Medicare/Fraud-and-Abuse/PhysicianSelfReferral/advisory_opinions.html.

legal authority, it would be exceedingly difficult for a whistleblower to make out a knowing Stark violation with respect to an arrangement that is on all fours with an arrangement that received a favorable advisory opinion.

As noted above and in various places throughout this book, CMS has published certain FAQs on its website.[8] It is important to make note of and copy FAQs when they appear, because some may disappear from the website, and not necessarily because they do not reflect current CMS policy. FAQs are informal guidance that are not binding on CMS, but may be especially useful when structuring an arrangement, and may help to combat a claim of a knowing Stark violation (or conversely, could be used by a relator or the Department of Justice (DOJ) to claim that a physician or entity was put on notice that its conduct was prohibited by Stark).[9]

C. Case Law

In addition to the Stark Law, the Stark Regulations, and advisory opinions, there is also limited case law interpreting the scope, application, and enforceability of all aspects of the Stark Law. Unfortunately, the case law is of limited utility because relatively few cases are filed and brought to a final decision. CMS does no affirmative enforcement of Stark, and there is no private right of action to enforce Stark in the context of claims denials only. Rather, Stark is enforced solely through FCA cases brought by relators or the DOJ (and self-disclosures, which are discussed in the next chapter). Most of these cases are either settled or dismissed. For those cases that proceed to an endpoint through actual litigation, the courts typically have addressed only limited aspects of the Stark Law, and sometimes misinterpret its complex requirements and related guidance. The Supreme Court has not yet weighed in on a Stark question to create national

8 *See* https://www.cms.gov/Medicare/Fraud-and-Abuse/PhysicianSelfReferral/Downloads/FAQs-Physician-Self-Referral-Law.pdf.

9 In this regard, note that the 2018 "Brand Memo" (entitled "Limiting Use of Agency Guidance Documents in Affirmative Civil Enforcement Cases"), which, as its title suggests, appeared to restrict the use of sub-regulatory guidance as a means for proving a FCA violation, was rescinded by DOJ in 2021. *See* https://www.justice.gov/opa/page/file/1408606/download.

precedent. Nonetheless, there appears to be an increasing amount of case law in recent years, and certain cases are worth noting.

It is important to remember that the 2020 final rule made significant changes to the Stark regulations, including adding rules for when compensation takes into account the volume or value of referrals or other business generated, and a significantly revised definition of "indirect compensation arrangement." Therefore, due to changes made by the 2020 final rule as well as other regulatory changes, some of the caselaw discussed below may not be of continuing applicability. However, given the six-year lookback period for purposes of the 60-day rule and the six to 10 year statute of limitations for the FCA, cases decided prior to the effective date of the 2020 final rule may continue to live on for quite some time regardless of whether the points of law at issue in them have changed prospectively.

1. U.S. ex rel. Drakeford v. Tuomey Healthcare System

In this case Tuomey Health System paid $72.4 million to resolve a $237 million jury verdict that was upheld by the Fourth Circuit. In May 2013, the jury in *Tuomey* returned a verdict finding that the defendant, Tuomey Health System (Tuomey), violated the Stark Law and the False Claims Act through certain indirect compensation arrangements with physicians, leading to $39 million in impermissible claims to Medicare.[10]

In *Tuomey,* Tuomey Healthcare System created a for-profit entity for the purposes of owning four limited liability companies that employed physicians part-time to provide certain outpatient surgeries and other procedures constituting designated health services. The physicians received salaries and performance incentives greater than the amounts the LLCs received for the procedures performed by those physicians. The physicians' employment agreements required that the physicians perform the covered procedures *exclusively* at Tuomey facilities, and stipulated that they were employees only during the time that they were performing the procedures. In addition to the payment for the procedures (the professional component), Tuomey also received payment for the technical fee (facility fee) associated

[10] *See U. S. ex rel. Drakeford v. Tuomey*, 976 F. Supp. 2d 776 (D.S.C. 2013).

with each procedure. The physicians received significant compensation from Tuomey that (through performance incentives) varied with the volume of referrals to Tuomey.

The government alleged that, in total through these LLC arrangements, Tuomey was losing between $1 and $2 million per year and that Tuomey would not have entered such arrangements without the additional revenue generated from the associated improper referrals to Tuomey.

Originally, the district judge imposed a $45 million penalty against Tuomey. The Fourth Circuit Court of Appeals overturned the judgment on procedural grounds (7th Amendment right to a jury trial).[11] In reversing the district court, the Fourth Circuit addressed certain Stark Law issues in greater detail. Specifically, under the Stark Law, the Fourth Circuit held that: (1) a "referral" is generated in the context of inpatient and outpatient hospital services even when a physician personally performs the service because of the technical component of the service; and (2) contracts that value anticipated future referrals implicate the volume or value prohibition.

The case is perhaps best known, however, for the Fourth Circuit's 2015 opinion[12] and its surprisingly erroneous discussion concerning compensation based on personally performed services. Because personally performed services are neither referrals for DHS nor "other business generated," compensation that is based on personally performed services cannot take into account the volume or value of referrals or other business generated. However, the court noted that the physicians' personally performed services were accompanied by referrals for DHS, namely the facility services the hospital billed for in conjunction with the physicians' procedures. Tuomey had argued that preamble language in the Phase II final rule made clear that the "fact that corresponding hospital services are billed would not invalidate an employed physician's personally performed work, for which the physician may be paid a productivity bonus (subject to the fair market value requirement)."[13] But the court maintained that (1) the

---

[11] *U. S. ex rel. Drakeford v. Tuomey Healthcare Sys., Inc.*, 675 F.3d 394 (4th Cir. 2012).

[12] *Id. at* 792 F. 3d 364 (4th Cir. 2015).

[13] *See* 69 Fed. Reg. at 16089.

Phase II statement dealt only with a productivity bonus and not with a physician's base salary, and (2) the Phase II commentary was directed at the exception for bona fide employment relationships. Both points made by the court are differences without a distinction. As for the hospital's argument that the commentary applies irrespective of whether a bona fide employment relationship exists, the court boldly claimed that "[n]othing in the statute or the regulations, however, supports this notion."[14] Actually, the Phase I and Phase II commentary are clear that the volume or value analysis is the same for all exceptions.[15]

In any event, CMS has clearly repudiated *Tuomey's* conclusions on this issue by acknowledging *Tuomey's* discussion and by going to considerable lengths in reaffirming its Phase II analysis in the 2020 final rule.[16]

2. U.S. ex rel. Singh v. Bradford Regional Medical Center[17]

Bradford serves as an example both of the care entities must use in valuing arrangements implicating the Stark Law and of the difficulties courts have in analyzing Stark issues. Specifically, the arrangement that the court found violated the Stark Law was between a physician-owned medical practice and Bradford Regional Medical Center (Bradford). Under the arrangement at issue, Bradford subleased a nuclear camera from the medical practice, which was used to perform diagnostic tests constituting DHS. Although this agreement did not require the physicians to refer patients to Bradford for the diagnostic testing, the evidence showed that the parties anticipated these referrals when setting the compensation under the arrangement. For example, prior to the arrangement the physicians accounted for nearly half of such referrals to Bradford. Under the arrangement at issue, Bradford paid the medical practice a fixed "pass-through"

---

[14] *See* 792 F.3d at 380, n.10.

[15] *See* 66 Fed. Reg. at 867; 69 Fed. Reg. at 16068.

[16] *See* 85 Fed. Reg. at 77539.

[17] *U. S. ex rel. Singh v. Bradford Reg'l Med. Ctr.*, 752 F. Supp. 2d 602 (W.D. Pa., 2010).

amount for the lease, as well as a fixed fee for a non-compete portion of the agreement.

The court's Stark analysis is detailed and interesting in some respects. The court concluded that the lease was an indirect compensation arrangement between Bradford and the medical practice. Although the fees paid by Bradford were "fixed," the court concluded that the manner in which the fees took into account the volume or value of referrals because the fee was based on a calculation of expected revenues with the lease in place, less expected revenues without the lease in place. In an apparent conflation of the concept of volume or value of referrals with that of fair market value, the court found that this arrangement did not meet the definition of fair market value for purposes of the exception for indirect compensation arrangements because the fee valued anticipated referrals. The court did not appreciate that fair market value and taking into account the volume or value of referrals are two separate concepts.[18]

The case is also notable for the fact that the hospital's fair market appraisal was not done by a health care appraisal firm. A health care appraisal expert, if consulted, might have advised that a non-compete arrangement that takes into consideration lost revenue from a referral source that would otherwise be a competitor is inherently risky.

3. U.S. ex rel. Bookwalter v. UPMC

In this case, the Third Circuit issued a decision in September 2019[19] and, following its grant of a petition for rehearing, modified it in December 2019.[20] The September 2019 decision is notable for three

---

[18] To illustrate, suppose two executives within the same hospital propose to lease space to two group practices for the exact same size office space that are located next to each other in the same building, with the same amenities, and under the same terms, etc. The first executive pays no attention to past or anticipated referrals and sets the price per square foot for Group 1's space at $x. The second executive, wanting to reward Group 2 for its past referrals and in anticipation of future referrals, also sets the price at $x. Either both executives are correct that $x is fair market value, or both are incorrect, but it cannot be that one is correct and the other incorrect.

As noted above at B.2. of Chapter 2, in the 2020 final rule, CMS struck the reference to volume or value of referrals from the definition of fair market value.

[19] *U. S. ex rel. Bookwalter v. UPMC*, 938 F.3d 397 (3d. Cir. 2019).

[20] *U. S. ex rel. Bookwalter v. UPMC*, 946 F.3d 162 (3d Cir. 2019).

reasons. First, the panel found that because the relator adequately pled an indirect compensation arrangement between the referring physicians and the medical center, it was entitled to discovery.[21] Stark is structured so that if there is a financial relationship between a physician who refers DHS to an entity, a prima facie violation has occurred, and it is up to the defendant to provide the existence of an exception.[22] Notwithstanding that the case before it was brought under the FCA, and that the Government normally has the burden to prove each element of a FCA violation, including falsity and knowledge that the claim was false, the Court reasoned that its job is to gauge whether a complaint states a "plausible" claim to relief, and whereas plausible does not mean merely possible, it also does not mean probable. The Court further stated that its job is not to dismiss claims that it may think will fail in the end, but instead, the court asks only if it has enough facts to raise a reasonable expectation that discovery will reveal evidence of each element. In response to the concern raised by the concurring judge that the type of relative value units (RVU)-based compensation at issue was a very common methodology and that the majority's approach could lead to frivolous suits brought against hospitals, the majority stated that courts are only the second-line defense against frivolous lawsuits behind the DOJ, which can dismiss frivolous whistleblower defenses over the objections of the relator.[23]

Second, the panel concluded that the "aggregate compensation" element of the indirect compensation arrangement definition was satisfied. The panel reasoned that: (1) although the physicians' procedures performed at the hospital were "personally performed services" and thus not "referrals" within the meaning of the Stark regulations; (2) inpatient and outpatient hospital services *are* DHS; and (3) therefore, because the physicians received productivity bonuses after reaching a certain level of RVUs, all else being equal, the more procedures the

---

[21] In response to this holding, CMS made it more difficult, in the 2020 final rule, for an indirect compensation arrangement to arise by significantly increasing the definitional requirements for an indirect compensation arrangement.

[22] *U. S. ex rel. Kosenske v. Carlisle HMA, Inc.* , 554 F.3d 88, 95 (3d Cir. 2009).

[23] In this regard the majority was either disingenuous or naive. Although the number of DOJ dismissals of qui tam complaints may have increased slightly in the past few years, dismissals remain relatively rare, even in weak cases.

physicians referred to the hospitals, the more RVUs they accumulated and the higher their aggregate compensation.

Third, the panel found that the physicians' "suspiciously high" compensation suggested that the compensation took into account the volume or value of referrals, and cited to the Phase II commentary that said that even fixed compensation may take into account the volume or value of referrals if it is inflated beyond fair market value for that purpose.[24] The 2020 final rule put an end to this theory, at least prospectively, by providing that in order for compensation to take into account the volume or value of referrals the compensation formula itself must establish a positive or negative correlation.[25]

In the December 2019 modified opinion, the panel withdrew its language in the previous opinion that held that, for purposes of the aggregate compensation element of the definition of "indirect compensation arrangement," the relator plausibly pled that the physicians' compensation "varied with" the volume or value of referrals to the medical center. However, the court found that the relator plausibly pled that the physicians' compensation "took into account" their referrals for purposes of the aggregate compensation element.[26]

The December 2019 opinion also reiterated that the relator did not bear the burden of pleading that no Stark exception exists, but rather the defendant bears the burden of pleading that a Stark exception exists. The court noted the medical center's "simple and cogent" logic that, in an FCA case the plaintiff bears the burden of proving each element of an FCA violation, including falsity, but said its precedent (namely, *Kosenske*, discussed below) compelled that it reject that argument.

4. U.S. ex rel. Kosenske v. Carlisle HMA Inc. et al.[27]

Kosenske presents another example of the importance of good evidence to support a fair market value determination under the Stark Law. *Kosenske* considered remuneration in the context of

---

[24] *See* 938 F.3d at 412, citing 69 Fed. Reg. at 16059.

[25] *See* 85 Fed. Reg at 77537 (middle column).

[26] Although some have criticized the September 2019 opinion's analysis of the "varies with" analysis because it focused on personally performed services, the author believes it is correct.

[27] *U. S. ex rel. Kosenske v. Carlisle HMA Inc.*, 554 F.3d 88 (3d Cir. 2009).

physician-hospital arrangements. The Third Circuit Court of Appeals held that an arrangement between an anesthesiology provider group and a hospital did not meet the requirements of the exception for PSAs in part, because the parties did not satisfy the fair market value requirement and did not have a written arrangement for all items and services to be provided. Although the parties argued that their initial contract negotiations were adequate evidence that the agreement reflected fair market value, and although the district court below accepted this argument, the Third Circuit rejected this argument, finding the fact that an arrangement is negotiated back and forth between the parties does not, per se, cause an arrangement to meet the Stark Law definition of fair market value. This decision emphasizes the importance of appropriately documenting (and updating documentation of) all aspects of arrangements implicating the Stark Law, including detailed evidence and support for the fair market value of the remuneration to be exchanged pursuant to an agreement.

The *Kosenske* court also held that once the plaintiff proves a prima facie case of a Stark violation (i.e., a financial relationship between a referring physician and an entity, and a referral for DHS by such physician to the entity), the defendant bears the burden of proving an exception. This allocation of the burden of proof makes sense in a case involving only claims liability,[28] but the court did not explain why this should be true in an FCA case, where traditionally the plaintiff has borne the burden of proving each element of a valid FCA claim, including falsity. If a Stark exception applies, the claim is not false.[29]

Finally, this case might have turned out quite differently if the district court was made aware that, under the Stark rules at the time, there may not have been a compensation arrangement between the parties. The PSA and the referrals at issue occurred well before the adoption of the stand-in-the-shoes rule in the Phase III final rule. Therefore, unless the physicians signed the PSA in their individual

---

28 In fact, the regulations codify this allocation. *See* 42 C.F.R. § 411.353(c)(2)(i).

29 Instead, the *Kosenske* court simply cited a district court decision from outside the Third Circuit, which in turn provided no analysis and which cited a district court decision that did not involve or even mention Stark. *See U. S. ex rel. Kosenske v. Carlisle HMA Inc.*, 554 F.3d at 96, citing *U. S. v. Rogan*, 459 F. Supp. 2d 692, 716 (N.D. Ill. 2006) (citing *U. S. v. Shaw*, 106 F. Supp. 2d 103, 122 (D. Mass. 2000)).

capacity, there was not a direct compensation arrangement, and probably not an indirect compensation arrangement between the referring physicians and the hospital. Apparently this was overlooked by the hospital's original counsel, but was discovered by counsel that represented the hospital in the district court after the remand ordered by the Third Circuit. However, the district court would not consider counsel's arguments on this point, instead finding that the question of whether there was a financial arrangement was foreclosed by the mandate issued by the Third Circuit.[30]

5. U.S. ex rel. Goodstein v. McLaren Regional Medical Center[31]

Goodstein is unusual because the sole issue in this intervened FCA case was fair market value. The Government claimed that Goodstein knowingly paid above fair market value for space it leased from a physician group in a scheme to reward referrals from the group's physicians. The case was a battle of the experts, with three experts testifying on behalf of the defendants and two testifying on behalf of the Government. The court found that the defendants' experts were more credible and persuasive than the Government's experts. The flaws the court found in the Government's experts' reports were: (1) the failure to consider relevant comparable buildings; (2) a too restrictive market area; and (3) not properly adjusting the analysis for the specific terms of McClaren's lease.[32] The court noted that one of the defendant's experts had prepared a fair market value appraisal prior to any litigation (including litigation before a tax tribunal) concerning the property.[33] The court also took into consideration several issues the parties haggled over during negotiations, and gave examples of favorable provisions that were requested by the physicians and rejected by McClaren.[34] The court concluded that the lease agreement at issue was an arm's length transaction, the rental

---

30 *See U. S. ex rel. Kosenske v. Carlisle HMA, Inc.*, 2010 U.S. Dist. LEXIS 31619 at *19 (M.D. Pa. 2010).

31 *U. S. ex rel. Goodstein v. McLaren Reg'l Med. Ctr.*, 202 F. Supp. 2d 671 (E.D. Mich. 2002).

32 *See* 202 F. Supp. 2d at 685-86.

33 *See id.* at 685.

34 *See id.* at 676-77.

rate was consistent with fair market value, and that there was no evidence that the rental rate was determined in a manner that took into account the value of potential referrals.[35]

6. U.S. ex rel. Villafane v. Solinger[36]

Villafane is notable both because it is one of few if any cases addressing the academic medical center exception to the Stark Law as well as for two basic errors the court made in its analysis.

First, it appears that this FCA should have been dismissed by the court. The *Villafane* court bizarrely brought Medicaid claims under the ambit of the Stark Law's prohibition on payment of Medicare DHS furnished pursuant to a non-compliant financial relationship. In its decision, the court noted that the parties acknowledged that the claims at issue involved only Medicaid (not Medicare) funds but instead of dismissing the case, it stated that this fact did not impact the court's analysis of the case.[37] Although it is true that once there has been a referral of Medicare DHS that does not meet a Stark exception, the entity may not bill Medicare or any other payor (including Medicaid),[38] that does not change the basic fact that there must be a tainted referral for Medicare DHS in the first place for the claims payment prohibition to arise.[39]

---

35 The court stated, without explanation, that the Government had the burden to show that the rental charges took into account the volume or value of referrals. *See id.* at 686. Thus one cannot discern whether the court placed the burden of proof on the Government because the case before it was an FCA case, or whether it was referring to the alleged AKS violation as opposed to the alleged Stark violation, or some other reason. As noted above, *Kosenske* and *Bookwalter* placed the burden of proof on the defendant to show the absence of a Stark violation. The court's opinion is not clear as to which party, if either, had the burden on the issue of fair market value.

36 *U. S. ex rel. Villafane v. Solinger*, 543 F. Supp. 2d 678 (W.D. Ky. 2008).

37 543 Supp. 2d at 681, n.3.

38 *See* section 1877(a)(1)(B) of the Social Security Act, 42 U.S.C. § 1395nn(a)(1)(B).

39 To clarify, referrals of only *Medicare* DHS are subject to the payment prohibition due to a non-excepted financial relationship. However, section 1903 of the Social Security Act, 42 U.S.C. § 1396b, provides that no Federal Financial Participation (FFP) may be paid by the Secretary to a State for Medicaid DHS, that, had they been Medicare DHS, would not be payable due to noncompliance with Stark. *See* discussion of the *Halifax* decision below.

Second, the court concluded that the AMC exception was applicable despite the referrals at issue apparently having taken place before the effective date of the exception. In an earlier opinion, the court reasoned that the AMC was nevertheless applicable because the exception merely "serves as an administrative interpretation of the meaning Congress intended when creating the statute."[40] The court either ignored or did not understand that the AMC exception was created by CMS using its authority under section 1877(b)(4) of the Social Security Act to create new exceptions, and that the exception was made effective for referrals on or after January 4, 2002.[41]

With respect to the merits, the court took a pragmatic approach to the AMC exception. In particular, the court was willing to overlook potential technical issues, including inaccurate timekeeping by faculty physicians, compensation to physicians at above the 75th percentile, and lack of detailed contracts documenting certain relationships between the relevant parties. Instead, the court focused on the overarching purpose of the Stark Law in preventing fraud and abuse.

7. U.S. ex rel. Baklid-Kunz v. Halifax Hospital Medical Center

According to the relator, Halifax Hospital entered into employment agreements with several outside physicians that allegedly took the volume or value of referrals into account in setting the level of compensation paid to the physicians. The physicians received incentive compensation from a pool of funds that was divided among the physicians. In the complaint, the relator alleged that the physicians increased referrals in order to maximize the potential bonus because more patients meant a large potential pool.

In its decision, the Court held that Halifax violated Stark by paying incentive bonuses that improperly took the volume or value of referrals for DHS or other business generated into account.[42] Halifax argued in vain that the incentive bonus was based upon services personally performed by the physicians, which is allowable under the

---

[40] *U. S. v. Solinger*, 457 F. Supp. 2d 743, 756 (W.D. Ky. 2006).

[41] *See* 66 Fed. Reg. at 856.

[42] *U.S. ex rel Baklid-Kunz v. Halifax Hospital Medical Center*, 2013 WL 6017329 (M.D. Fla. 2013).

bona fide employment exception, which permits productivity bonuses that do not take into account, directly or indirectly, the volume or value of referrals. However, the Court correctly accepted the government's argument that the bonus was *based* upon factors beyond just a physician's personally performed services, although the bonus was *divided* according to personally performed services. The Court specifically took issue with the fact that the bonus pool included DHS.[43] Accordingly, the Court held that Halifax violated Stark.

Halifax is also notable for its ruling concerning the connection between Stark and Medicaid.[44] In its motion to dismiss, Halifax argued that Stark could not serve as the basis for a claim under the FCA concerning the allegedly improper Medicaid claims and reimbursements. In denying the motion to dismiss, the Court correctly determined that the Medicaid statute prohibits States from receiving Federal Financial Participation (FFP) for Medicaid services that were furnished pursuant to a referral that violate Stark if the service were a Medicare DHS.[45] Of course, the court's ruling means only that the Government's theory that Halifax caused the State to submit false claims was viable (assuming the claims were false). The Government would still need to prove that the hospital *knowingly* caused the State to submit false claims. Moreover a defendant in this type of claim would seem to have a good argument that any alleged claim that the provider or supplier caused the State to falsely claim FFP was not material to CMS's decision to pay FFP. To the best of the author's knowledge, CMS has never taken back FFP from a State due to section 1903(s) of the Act, and it obviously is aware that,

---

[43] In other words, because the bonus pool included DHS it did not matter how it was distributed because, all else being equal, the more DHS a physician ordered the greater the bonus pool and the greater the distribution to the physician. Because the distribution was based on each physician's personally performed services, the compensation methodology only *indirectly* took into account the volume or value of referrals for DHS, but most exceptions that have a volume-or-value prohibition, including the exception for bona fide employment arrangements, which is what was at issue in *Halifax*, prohibit a direct or indirect taking into account the volume or value of referrals.

[44] *U.S. ex rel Baklid-Kunz v. Halifax Hosp. Med. Ctr.*, 2012 WL 921147 (M.D. Fla. 2012).

[45] *U. S. ex rel. Baklid-Kunz v. Halifax Hosp. Med. Ctr.*, 2012 U.S. Dist. LEXIS 36304 (M.D. Fla. 2012).

when a hospital or other entity makes a self-disclosure under the Self-Referral Disclosure Protocol (SRDP) for Medicare services that were referred by physicians with a non-excepted financial relationship, the same physicians also referred Medicaid services. This *Halifax* ruling has been followed by two other district courts.[46]

[46] *U.S. ex rel. Schubert v. All Children's Medical Center, Inc.*, 2013 U.S. Dist. LEXIS 163075 (M.D. Fla. Nov. 15, 2013); *U.S. ex rel. Parikh v. Citizens Medical Center*, 2013 U.S. Dist. LEXIS 134693 (S.D. Tex. Sept. 20, 2013).

6
Penalties and Compromise

OUTLINE

Stark violations carry serious consequences ranging from the denial of claims to civil monetary penalties to potential exclusion from participation in federal health care programs.

A. Claims Denials

The basic penalty in the Stark statute is the denial of claims submitted (and perhaps already paid) pursuant to a tainted referral/financial relationship. The statute commands that "[n]o payment may be made under this title for a designated health service which is provided in violation of subsection (a)(1)."[1] Thus, the statute does not provide the Secretary with the discretion to deny or not deny claims submitted

[1] Section 1877(g)(1) of the Social Security Act, 42 U.S.C. § 1395nn(g)(1).

in violation of Stark. The mandatory denial of claims language, combined with the fact that Stark is a strict liability statute, and taking into consideration that an arrangement that has been incorrectly structured may relate to dozens of physicians and last several years, means that in many cases the potential claims liability is staggering. However, in 2010 the ACA required the Secretary to develop a mechanism for compromising the amount of claims liability for putative Stark violations. In response, CMS developed the Self-Referral Disclosure Protocol, which is discussed below.

In addition to the mandatory claims denial language, the statute provides that if a claim submitted in violation of the law is paid in error, any co-pays associated with that claim must be refunded to the beneficiary.[2]

B. Sanctions Beyond Claims Denials

Where a knowing Stark violation has occurred, the HHS Office of the Inspector General (OIG) may seek to impose civil monetary penalties (CMPs) of up to $15,000 per improper claim and may exclude the offending physician and/or the DHS entity (depending on which party or parties had knowledge of the violation) from participation in federal health care programs.[3] Anyone who enters into an arrangement or scheme that he or she knows has a principal purpose of circumventing the Stark Law is subject to civil monetary penalties of up to $100,000 per scheme and exclusion from federal health care programs.[4] An entity that furnishes Medicare services and, upon request from CMS or the OIG, fails to report relevant information regarding its financial relationships is subject to a penalty of $10,000 per day for each day the failure to report continues.[5] Such failure also may be grounds for exclusion from federal health care programs.

---

2 Section 1877(g)(1) of the Social Security Act, 42 U.S.C. § 1395nn(g)(2). See also 42 C.F.R. § 411.353(d) ("An entity that collects payment for a designated health service that was performed pursuant to a prohibited referral must refund all collected amounts on a timely basis, as defined at § 1003.101 of this title").

3 Section 1877(g)(3) of the Social Security Act, 42 U.S.C. § 1395nn(g)(3).

4 Section 1877(g)(4) of the Social Security Act, 42 U.S.C. § 1395nn(g)(4).

5 Section 1877(g)(5) of the Social Security Act, 42 U.S.C. § 1395nn(g)(5).

The statute also provides for CMP liability for the failure to refund co-pays.[6] The OIG's regulations require that co-pays be refunded on a "timely basis" and defines "timely basis" as "the 60-day period from the time the prohibited amounts are collected by the individual or the entity."[7] To date, there do not appear to be any CMPs issued for failure to make refunds.

C. False Claims Act Liability

The FCA generally prohibits knowingly presenting or causing to be presented a false or fraudulent claim for payment by the federal government.[8] Knowing and intentional violations of Stark may lead to FCA liability. Parties that have allegedly intentionally set-up arrangements to circumvent Stark or to directly not comply have been found liable under the FCA for submitting false or fraudulent claims that arose from those arrangements. Because CMS does virtually no affirmative enforcement of the Stark statute, the FCA (along with self-enforcement in the form of self-disclosures) is the principal means of enforcement.

The ACA created another means of imposing FCA liability for a Stark violation. Section 6402 of the ACA requires a party to report and return an overpayment by the later of (1) sixty days of identifying the overpayment or (2) the date a corresponding cost report is due. An overpayment consists of any funds paid under a federal health care program to which the receiving entity or individual is not entitled. Given the mandatory claims denial language of the statute, any payment for Medicare DHS received and retained pursuant to a noncompliant relationship or arrangement results in the receipt of overpayments.

On February 16, 2016, CMS published the final rule implementing the overpayment return requirement.[9] As under the ACA, the final rule requires the return of overpayments within sixty days of identification. The final rule provides that a person has identified an

---

[6] Section 1877(g)(3) of the Social Security Act, 42 U.S.C. § 1395nn(g)(3).

[7] 42 C.F.R. §§1003.300, 1003.110.

[8] 31 U.S.C. §§ 3729-3733.

[9] 81 Fed. Reg. 7654.

overpayment when the person has, or should have through the exercise of reasonable diligence, determined that the person has received an overpayment and quantified the amount of the overpayment. The final rule's reasonable diligence standard[10] is easier to satisfy (and thus less kind) than what was contained in the proposed rule. The proposed rule proposed that an overpayment was identified if the person has actual knowledge of the existence of the overpayment or acts in reckless disregard or deliberate ignorance of the existence of the overpayment.[11] One court has characterized the final rule's reasonable diligence standard as a negligence standard that is inconsistent with the FCA's knowing standard, and also held that the adoption of the reasonable diligence standard violated the Administrative Procedure Act's requirement that a final rule be the logical outgrowth of a proposed rule.[12] On appeal, the Secretary did not challenge these holdings of the district court, but the case was reversed on other grounds.[13]

On the other hand, the final rule's requirement that an overpayment has been identified when it has been quantified,[14] is decidedly advantageous to providers and suppliers. Surely, one cannot deliberately fail to quantify an overpayment and then claim protection under the rule, but the preamble to the final rule explains that one has conducted reasonable diligence if it has concluded its investigation of credible information of a potential overpayment within six months (at the most), except in "extraordinary circumstances."[15]

---

[10] See id. at 7661-68, codified at 42 C.F.R. § 401.305(a)(2).

[11] *See* 77 Fed. Reg. at 9187.

[12] *UnitedHealthcare Ins. Co. v. Azar*, 330 F. Supp. 3d 173, 191-192 (D.D.C. 2018).

[13] *UnitedHealthcare Ins. Co. v. Becerra*, 16 F.4th 867, 881 (D.C. Cir. 2021). Note that in response to the district court's decision, CMS issued a proposed rule on December 27, 2022, in which it proposed that a person has identified an overpayment when the person knowingly receives or retains an overpayment. The term "knowingly" would have the meaning set forth in 31 U.S.C. 3729(b)(1)(A). That section of the False Claims Act defines "knowingly" as any circumstance in which "a person, with respect to information—(i) has actual knowledge of the information; (ii) acts in deliberate ignorance of the truth or falsity of the information; or (iii) acts in reckless disregard of the truth or falsity of the information." *See* 87 Fed. Reg. at 79559-60, 79699.

[14] *See* 81 Fed. Reg. at 7654, 7661, 7663-64.

[15] *See id.* at 7662. The six months/extraordinary circumstances standard is not codified.

CMS declined to define "extraordinary circumstances" but said that they "may include unusually complex investigations that the provider or supplier reasonably anticipates will require more than six months to investigate, such as physician self-referral law violations that are referred to the CMS Voluntary Self-Referral Disclosure Protocol (SRDP)." The final rule contains a six-year look-back period for any overpayments, which exceeds the four-year reopening period for Medicare claims payments that were not fraudulently obtained and arguably is in conflict with the reopening regulation.[16]

D. Self-Referral Disclosure Protocol

Section 6409 of the ACA created a Stark-specific Self-Referral Disclosure Protocol (SRDP) to allow parties to voluntarily report a Stark violation to CMS.[17] The SRDP was necessary for a number of reasons. For instance, the OIG, on May 29, 2009, stopped accepting into its self-disclosure protocol Stark violations that were unaccompanied by a colorable violation of the Anti-Kickback Statute,[18] which left parties without a clear avenue to self-report and resolve a Stark violation.

The purpose of the SRDP is to provide a procedure whereby Stark violations can be self-disclosed and the disclosing party can work with CMS to resolve the violation. As enacted in the Affordable Care Act, CMS has discretion to reduce the possible penalties associated with the disclosed Stark violation. The SRDP is for Stark violations only, not violations of any other law. If a party believes an arrangement may also involve a violation of the Anti-Kickback Statute or

---

[16] Regulation 42 C.F.R. § 401.305(f) provides that an "overpayment" must be reported and returned within 6 years of the date the overpayment was received, but section 401.303 defines an "overpayment" as funds to which one is not entitled. Under 42 C.F.R. § 405.980(b), after four years, an entity is entitled to keep funds the entity incorrectly, but not fraudulently, received. So if the entity discovers after four years the receipt of such funds, the entity is entitled to keep such funds under section 405.980(b) but not under section 401.305(f).

[17] Section 6409 of the ACA required the Department of Health and Human Services to promulgate the SRDP.

[18] It was also questionable whether the OIG had authority to resolve a suspected Stark violation given the strict liability nature of the statute and the fact that CMS retains authority for its claims determinations.

some other law, the disclosure should occur elsewhere, such as the OIG or Department of Justice. Further, the SRDP is not part of CMS's advisory opinion process, which means that submissions should only be made for actual violations.

Entering the SRDP program stays a party's obligation to return suspected overpayments. Specifically, once a submission is accepted by CMS, the sixty-day period for returning overpayments created by Section 6402 of the Affordable Care Act is stayed. The stay continues so long as the party remains in the SRDP. This can be beneficial because CMS's ability to compromise the amount owed may enable a party to avoid returning the full amount resulting from a violation, depending upon the factors identified below.

CMS promulgated the initial SRDP on September 23, 2010, with technical corrections made on May 6, 2011. The SRDP sets forth the requirements for a submission into the program. Beginning June 1, 2017, providers of services and suppliers must use the forms included in the OMB-approved collection instrument entitled CMS Voluntary Self-Referral Disclosure Protocol (SRDP) in order to utilize the SRDP.[19] For disclosures of noncompliant financial relationships with more than one physician, the disclosing entity must submit a separate Physician Information Form for each physician. The CMS Voluntary SRDP document contains one Physician Information Form. Additional stand-alone Physician Information Forms can be found in the links below. Specifically, an SRDP submission must include, among other things: (1) the names and identifying information of the disclosing party; (2) a description of the nature of the matter being disclosed; (3) a statement explaining why the disclosing party believes a violation of Stark occurred, including a legal analysis of each element of every applicable Stark exception; (4) how the matter was discovered and what, if any, remedial measures have been taken; (5) a description of the existence and adequacy of any pre-existing compliance program; (6) whether the disclosed conduct is under current investigation or inquiry by another government agency or contractor; (7) a financial analysis relating to the matter being disclosed;

---

[19] A new OMB-approved form became effective December 2022.

and (8) a signed certification from the chief executive officer, chief financial officer, or other authorized representative.[20]

Beginning March 1, 2023, for disclosures of noncompliance arising from the failure of a physician practice to qualify as a group practice under section 411.352, the self-disclosure must include: (1) the SRDP Disclosure Form; (2) the Group Practice Information Form; (3) a Financial Analysis Worksheet; and (4) an acceptable Certification. As stated above, CMS has the discretion to reduce penalties associated with self-disclosed conduct. When determining whether a reduction will occur, CMS may consider the following factors: "(1) the nature and extent of the illegal or improper practice; (2) the timeliness of the self-disclosure; (3) the cooperation in providing additional information related to the disclosure; (4) the litigation risk associated with the matter disclosed; and (5) the financial position of the disclosing party."[21]

CMS periodically posts settlements under the SRDP on its website. However, the information given is only on a yearly, aggregate basis (i.e., amounts per provider are not given and no provider is identified).[22]

---

[20] The full Self-Referral Disclosure Protocol is available on CMS's website at: http://www.cms.gov/Medicare/Fraud-and-Abuse/PhysicianSelfReferral/Downloads/6409_SRDP_Protocol.pdf.

[21] *Id.*

[22] *See* https://www.cms.gov/Medicare/Fraud-and-Abuse/PhysicianSelfReferral/Self_Referral_Disclosure_Protocol.

Resources and Reference Guide

Some of the resources that may assist in the interpretation and application of Stark are identified below.

A. ABA Health Law Section Resources

1. The Stark & Anti-Kickback Toolkit—The toolkit is an electronic searchable database that includes narrative summaries, statutes, administrative history, regulations, administrative materials, links to the CMS website for Stark advisory opinions, links to the OIG website for anti-kickback advisory opinions, and several ABA Health Law Section publications.
2. *The Health Lawyer*—A bimonthly scholarly publication analyzing a variety of issues in the health law field.
3. *Health eSource*—A monthly electronic publication with shorter articles analyzing issues in the health law field.
4. *Health Care Fraud and Abuse: Practical Perspectives*—A book containing an in-depth analysis of federal fraud and abuse laws and regulations, including analyses of specific issues.
5. Health Law Section Resources Page: https://www.americanbar.org/groups/health_law/events_cle/webinars/

B. Government Resources

1. Centers for Medicare and Medicaid Services: https://www.cms.gov
2. CMS Physician Self-Referral Webpage: https://www.cms.gov/Medicare/Fraud-and-Abuse/PhysicianSelfReferral/index.html
3. Office of the Inspector General of HHS: https://oig.hhs.gov

C. Federal Register Citations

The following is a mostly complete list of the Stark rules that have been published as of the date of publication of this book:[1]

- Stark I Proposed Rule—57 Fed. Reg. 8588 (Mar. 11, 1992)
- Stark I Final Rule—60 Fed. Reg. 41914 (Aug. 14, 1993)
- Stark II Proposed Rule—63 Fed. Reg. 1659 (Jan. 9, 1998)
- Stark II Phase I Final Rule—66 Fed. Reg. 856 (Jan. 4, 2001)
- Stark II Phase II Interim Final Rule—69 Fed. Reg. 16054 (Mar. 26, 2004)
- CY 2008 Physician Fee Schedule—72 Fed. Reg. 38122 (July 12, 2007)
- Stark II Phase III Final Rule—72 Fed. Reg. 51012 (Sept. 5, 2007)
- FY 2009 Inpatient Prospective Payment System Proposed Rule—73 Fed. Reg. 23528 (Apr. 30, 2008)
- FY 2009 Inpatient Prospective Payment System Final Rule—73 Fed. Reg. 48434 (Aug. 19, 2008)
- CY 2011 Outpatient Prospective Payment System Proposed Rule—75 Fed. Reg. 46431 (Aug. 3, 2010)
- CY 2011 Outpatient Prospective Payment System Final Rule—75 Fed. Reg. 71799 (Nov. 24, 2010)

---

[1] A complete list appears on CMS's website at https://www.cms.gov/Medicare/Fraud-and-Abuse/PhysicianSelfReferral/Significant-Regulatory-History. Of the rules listed above, the most significant are (in chronological order): the 1998 proposed rule; Phase I; Phase II; Phase III; the FY 2009 IPPS proposed and final rules; the CY 2016 PFS proposed and final rules; and the 2019 and 2020 Modernizing and Clarifying the Physician Self-Referral Regulations proposed and final rules.

- CY 2012 Outpatient Prospective Payment System Proposed Rule—76 Fed. Reg. 42349 (July 18, 2011)
- CY 2012 Outpatient Prospective Payment System Final Rule—76 Fed. Reg. 74517 (Nov. 30, 2011)
- CY 2016 Physician Fee Schedule Proposed Rule—80 FR 41685 (July 15, 2015)
- CY 2016 Physician Fee Schedule Final Rule—80 FR 70885 (Nov. 16, 2015)
- CY 2017 Physician Fee Schedule Proposed Rule—81 FR 46162 (July 15, 2016)
- CY 2017 Physician Fee Schedule Final Rule—81 FR 80170 (Nov. 15, 2016)
- Modernizing and Clarifying the Physician Self-Referral Regulations Proposed Rule—84 FR 55766 (Oct. 17, 2019)
- Modernizing and Clarifying the Physician Self-Referral Regulations Final Rule—85 FR 77492 (Dec. 2, 2020)

D. Case Citations

1. U. S. *ex rel.* Drakeford v. Tuomey Healthcare Sys., Inc., 675 F.3d 394 (4th Cir. 2012).
2. U. S. *ex rel.* Singh v. Bradford Reg'l Med. Ctr., 752 F. Supp. 2d 602 (W.D. Pa., 2010).
3. U. S. *ex rel.* Kosenske v. Carlisle HMA Inc. et al., 554 F.3d 88 (3rd Cir. 2009).
4. U. S. *ex rel.* Goodstein v. McLaren Regional Medical Center, 202 F. Supp. 2d 671 (E.D. Mich. 2002).
5. U. S. *ex rel.* Villafane v. Solinger, 543 F. Supp. 2d 678 (W.D. Ky. 2008).
6. U. S. *ex rel.* Bookwalter v. UPMC, 946 F.3d 162 (3d Cir. 2019.
7. U. S. *ex rel.* Baklid-Kunz v. Halifax Hosp. Med. Ctr., 2012 WL 921147 (M.D. Fla. 2012).

Appendix A: Decision Tree

When faced with a Stark issue for your organization or agency or for a client you represent, following a decision tree may be helpful. One such decision tree is the following:

Part 1—Is the statute implicated?

- Is there a physician somewhere in the mix?
- If no, Stark is not implicated.
- If yes, has the physician made a "referral"?
- If no, Stark is not implicated.
- If yes, is the referral for DHS?
- If no, Stark is not implicated.
- If yes, was the referral for DHS made to an "entity"?
- If no, Stark is not implicated.
- If yes, was there a "financial relationship" between the physician or immediate family member and the entity at the time the referral for DHS was made.
- If no, the statute is not implicated.
- If yes, the statute is implicated.

Part 2—Is the statute potentially violated?

- If the statute is implicated, is there an exception (general, ownership, or compensation) or other relief provided under the regulations that protects the referral or financial relationship?
- If yes, statute is not violated if there is a referral for DHS.

- If no, is there an applicable waiver?
- If yes, statute is not violated if there is a referral for DHS.
- If no, statute is violated if there is a referral for DHS.

Part 3—What are the consequences/actions parties should take if the statute is potentially violated?

- Has the entity billed "original Medicare" fee for service or any other payor or patient for DHS?
- If no, no refund responsibility, and, absent unusual circumstances, no other responsibility or sanction.
- If yes, refund responsibility may depend on when claim was made or paid and what payor was billed.
- Has the financial relationship between the referring physician and the entity ended or been brought into compliance?
- If yes, no additional action is necessary.
- If no, financial relationship should be terminated or brought into compliance.

The above does not purport to be the only or necessarily the best decision tree. Others may choose to start the analysis at a different point routinely (e.g., determining whether there is a "financial relationship" before determining whether there was a referral). Also, depending on the facts readily available to the practitioner in a particular situation, one may choose to jump ahead in the analysis and possibly end it without having all the facts. For example, if one does not yet know whether a particular service is DHS but knows that the physician does not have a direct or indirect financial relationship with an entity, there will not be a Stark violation if the physician refers DHS to the entity. Of course, even if one concludes at some point there is not a potential Stark violation, one may choose to dig deeper and evaluate whether some other statute may be violated (e.g., the Federal Anti-Kickback Statute, state self-referral or anti-kickback statute, fee-splitting statute, etc.).

Appendix B: ABA Recommendation to Congress on Amending the Stark Law

American Bar Association Health Law Section Report To The House Of Delegates

Resolution

RESOLVED, That the American Bar Association urges Congress to amend the Ethics in Patients Referrals Act of 1989, Section 1877 of the Social Security Act, 42 U.S.C. § 1395nn (commonly known as the "Stark Law"), to make changes to (a) clarify the application of the Stark Law and (b) address concerns of physicians and other health care providers that new alternative payment and delivery models promoted by the Centers for Medicare & Medicaid Services and other payers may result in violations of the Stark Law;

FURTHER RESOLVED, That the American Bar Association urges Congress to amend the Stark Law to remove the statutory prohibition against payment for services furnished pursuant to a compensation arrangement that failed to meet an exception to the Stark Law solely due to noncompliance with technical requirements of the statute;

FURTHER RESOLVED, That the American Bar Association urges Congress to amend the Stark Law to clarify the requirement that compensation must be consistent with fair market value, and to provide that a valuation from a nationally recognized health care appraiser or valuation consultant shall create a rebuttable presumption of fair market value for purposes of the Stark Law.

FURTHER RESOLVED, That the American Bar Association urges Congress to amend the Stark Law to provide greater clarity and consistency in the application of the prohibition on compensation arrangements that vary with or take into account the volume or value of physician referrals; and

FURTHER RESOLVED, That the American Bar Association urges Congress to adopt a statutory exception under the Stark Law for compensation paid under an alternative payment arrangement meeting specified requirements in order to encourage the adoption of collaborative health care delivery models without concerns of violating the Stark Law.

Report

Introduction

The purpose of this Resolution is to urge Congress to amend the Ethics in Patient Referrals Act, Section 1877 of the Social Security Act, 42 U.S.C. §1395nn (commonly known as the "Stark Law"), to provide clarification of critical requirements of the Stark Law and to address concerns of physicians and other health care providers who potentially face significant penalties under the Stark Law as a result of entering into collaborative health care delivery approaches and value-based incentive payment arrangements.

The Stark Law prohibits a physician from referring patients for *"designated health services"* ("DHS") payable by Medicare to an entity with which the physician or an immediate family member has a financial relationship, and prohibits the entity from submitting a claim for such DHS to Medicare, to the patient or to any other payer, unless an exception applies.[1] A financial relationship may be a direct or indirect ownership or investment interest, or a direct or indirect compensation arrangement. As more fully discussed below, the Stark Law is a strict liability law; if a financial relationship between a referring physician and an entity providing DHS is covered by the statute,

---

[1] Section 1903 of the Social Security Act, 42 U.S.C. §1396b, prohibits payment of the federal share of Medicaid to states for services paid under Medicaid that would have a constituted a prohibited referral under Medicare.

it must fit precisely within an exception to the statute or else the referral is prohibited and payment for the DHS is prohibited, without regard to the intent of the parties or the medical necessity of the DHS being provided.

Congress initially enacted the Stark Law in 1989 to prohibit physician referrals for clinical laboratory services covered by Medicare, unless an exception applied, to address concerns that physicians' financial relationships with clinical laboratories would unduly influence their clinical decision-making. In 1993, Congress expanded the definition of *"designated health services"* to include ten additional categories of DHS.

The categories of DHS subject to the Stark Law are: (1) clinical laboratory services; (2) physical therapy services; (3) occupational therapy services; (4) outpatient speech-language pathology services; (5) radiology and certain other imaging services; (6) radiation therapy services and supplies; (7) durable medical equipment and supplies; (8) parenteral and enteral nutrients, equipment and supplies; (9) prosthetics, orthotics, and prosthetic devices and supplies; (10) home health services; (11) outpatient prescription drugs; and (12) inpatient and outpatient hospital services.

There are over 30 exceptions to the Stark Law that are either included in the statutory language or that have been adopted by the Centers for Medicare & Medicaid Services ("CMS") in the Stark Law regulations. The Stark Law exceptions are divided into three categories: (1) general exceptions applying to both ownership and compensation arrangements; (2) exceptions applying only to ownership/investment interests; and (3) exceptions applying only to compensation arrangements. The exceptions to the Stark Law were intended to permit the existence of legitimate business relationships that would otherwise have been prohibited under the statute; however, several exceptions contain criteria that have become increasingly complex, inflexible and impractical to satisfy, especially in light of the significant changes in health care delivery and payment since the original adoption of the statute.

The Stark Law is considered to be a strict liability statute because no intent to violate the law is necessary for a violation to occur. If a financial or other arrangement between a physician and a DHS entity, such as a hospital, does not meet precisely all of the requirements of an exception, any payments received for any DHS furnished pursuant to a referral prohibited by the Stark Law must be refunded to Medicare or the applicable payer—regardless of whether the DHS were medically necessary and regardless of whether the non-compliance was highly technical, such as failure to timely sign a contract or other document involved in the arrangements. In addition, for "knowing" violations, the parties may be subject to enormous civil monetary penalties, as well as exclusion from participation in federal and state health care programs and liability under the False Claims Act.

In recent years, Congress has created alternative payment models, such as the Medicare Shared Savings Program, and has authorized the creation of other models in which payment for health care services is tied to a value-based methodology and not simply based on volume or the number of services provided. Indeed, there is near-universal agreement that great collaboration and coordination among health care providers is critical both for improving health outcomes and for controlling health care costs. However, health care providers have been hesitant to enter into collaborative health care service delivery arrangements and innovative payment arrangements for fear of violating the complex requirements of the Stark Law. Congress has authorized limited waivers from the Stark Law for the Medicare Shared Savings Program and has authorized CMS to create waivers for any alternative payment programs initiated through the Centers for Medicare and Medicaid Innovation ("CMMI"). However, these waivers of the Stark Law only apply to certain Medicare innovative payment models, may be of limited duration, and may not be issued until the model is underway. Outside of the very limited scope of arrangements that are covered by these waivers, the fear of inadvertently violating the Stark Law still inhibits the collaboration and cooperation among providers that our evolving health care policy otherwise encourages, even compels.

Current State of the Law and Proposals for Change

There have been few amendments to the Stark Law statute itself; however, CMS has done extensive rulemaking since 1989 to implement the statute as well as to create additional exceptions. The extensive regulatory changes by CMS have added to the complexity of the Stark Law and sometimes have been impediments to the development of value-based payment models that reward providers for delivering higher-quality and more cost-effective health care services. Notwithstanding this complexity, the Department of Justice and whistleblowers have brought False Claims Act cases on the theory that because (in their view) the statute is clear, the alleged Stark violations at issue must have been knowing violations.

The following sections identify some major areas where clarification of existing provisions of the Stark Law or amendments to those provisions would reduce the sometimes draconian effects of the law and reduce or eliminate impediments to the implementation of value-based delivery models and greater coordination of care without presenting a material risk of fraud, waste or other harm to the Medicare program.

"Technical" violations not causing program integrity concerns

Many of the regulations promulgated under the Stark Law involve formal, technical requirements, the failure to comply with which does not in and of itself pose any material risk of abuse to the Medicare program or its beneficiaries (e.g., payment of Medicare funds for services that were inappropriate or medically unnecessary). For example, the Stark Law exception for personal service arrangements between a referring physician and a DHS entity requires that the arrangement be reflected in a written agreement signed by the parties that is in place before any services are rendered or any compensation paid. If, through clerical error or unavoidable delays (e.g., a required signatory is on vacation or sick leave), a contract signature is delayed beyond the time permitted or omitted, any claims for services rendered before that deficiency is cured are prohibited, even if the claims were for appropriate, medically necessary items or services and even if Medicare would have paid the claims without question if the parties did not have a Stark-covered financial relationship. Similarly, if a written agreement for such an arrangement expires without being formally renewed but the parties nonetheless continue to perform in accordance with the contract, services rendered after the expiration date will give rise to a Stark Law violation, even if they would have been permissible if the parties had entered into a written extension.

Practitioners commonly refer to these types of violations as "technical" violations, because they do not result in claims to Medicare for items or services that are suspect from a program integrity standpoint (as distinguished from violations of the fair market value, commercial reasonableness and volume-or-value prohibition, which may indicate an arrangement that results in overutilization of services). However, CMS has consistently taken the position that there is no such thing as a technical Stark violation; any failure to meet the formal requirements of a Stark Law exception precisely is a violation subject to the same penalties as a failure to meet the substantive terms of an exception. Thus, the penalty for a late or missing signature on a contract is the same as the penalty that would apply if the contract provided for compensation that varied directly with the volume or value of referrals – any claim submitted to Medicare is prohibited by statute from being billed or paid, and the parties are subject both to repayment obligations and to penalties. In this context, the strict-liability nature of the Stark Law punishes both innocent errors and intentional misconduct with a sledgehammer approach.

Although CMS has offered some limited relief for temporary non-compliance with these sorts of formal requirements, that relief is quite narrow in scope. Given the ever-increasing complexities of the health care delivery system, the opportunity for non-substantive (technical) errors will likewise continue to increase. It is appropriate for the Stark Law to be amended to provide that the per se prohibition on payment for DHS referred under a financial relationship that does not meet all of the requirements of an exception does not apply to technical non-compliance with an exception. Such amendment would remove the threat of False Claims Act liability premised on the allegation by (chiefly) a relator or the Government that the technical non-compliance was a knowing violation, and would also obviate the legal obligation for a DHS entity that discovers the technical non-compliance to refund the payment for the DHS involved or, alternatively, to make a self-disclosure to CMS. Instead, such technical non-compliance would allow (but not require) CMS, upon audit, to deny payment retrospectively for such DHS if the DHS entity cannot establish that it met all technical requirements of an applicable exception.

Fair market value

A critical requirement of several exceptions to the Stark Law is that any compensation between a referring physician and a DHS entity must be "consistent with" fair market value; i.e., the Stark Law does not differentiate between arrangements in which the referring physician *pays* less than fair market value and those in which the referring physician *receives* less than fair market value. In contrast, for purposes of the Anti-Kickback Statute ("AKS"), 42 U.S.C. §1320a-7b(b),[2] the Government is rightly not concerned if the physician or other referral source is paid compensation that is less than fair market value, or conversely, pays the referral target in excess of fair market value. Accordingly, the ABA recommends that "consistent with fair market value" be clarified to mean that the referring physician *pays* at least fair market value for items and services furnished *by* a DHS entity and *receives* no more than fair market value for items and services provided *to* a DHS entity. (Thus, for example, a physician who rents office space from a DHS entity could not pay less than fair market value rent, and a hospital who contracts with a physician to provide medical direction services could not pay more than fair market value compensation for such services.)

The ABA also recommends that, in order to provide some assurance that the compensation paid or received will not be attacked by the Government or a relator as being more than or less than fair market value, where the parties to an arrangement secure a fair market valuation from an independent and competent valuator, that valuation should be presumed to be correct. This is especially important in the context of alternative payment arrangements in which the parties are attempting to arrive at the fair market value of a physician's success in lowering costs and increasing quality and patient satisfaction.

Volume or value of referrals

Generally, the Stark Law prohibits any payment that varies with or otherwise takes into account the volume or value of referrals from the recipient of the payment to the payer. The test for whether

---

[2] The AKS makes it a felony to offer, pay, solicit or receive any remuneration, in cash or in kind, for referring a person for items or services which may be paid for by any federal health care reimbursement program, such as Medicare, Medicaid and Tricare.

compensation impermissibly takes into account the volume or value of referrals has proven to be particularly vexing. For example, a hospital's payments to a physician for the bona fide performance of services may be considered by the Government or a relator to reflect the volume or value of referrals if the performing physician must admit a patient to a hospital in order to perform those services. The ABA recommends that Congress amend the Stark Law to clarify the interpretation and application of the "volume or value of referrals" prohibition in situations where there is ambiguity or inconsistency in the text of the statute or in the interpretations of the statute applied by CMS. The following paragraphs provides specific examples as to which the ABA believes amendments to the statute would provide greater clarity and consistency without undermining the policy goals of the Stark Law. Adoption of this Resolution will allow the ABA to address these and similar issues through appropriate outreach to Congress. First, the ABA recommends that Congress adopt the existing "safe harbor" in CMS's regulations for unit-based ("per click" or "per procedure") compensation and make it applicable through a statutory safe harbor to any type of compensation that is set in advance, including percentage compensation arrangements (e.g., compensation based on a percentage of revenue or percentage of collections). Such an amendment to the Stark Law would provide greater clarity to health care providers and would reduce the exposure of such providers to enforcement actions based on inconsistent interpretations of the Stark Law. For example, the ABA is aware of one case in which a health system was leveraged into a $25 million settlement because its percentage compensation arrangement was disallowed as taking into account the volume or value of referrals. Although CMS agrees that percentage compensation arrangements can meet its definition of "set in advance," and although the preamble language to CMS's regulations concerning the volume or value prohibition supported the health system's position, the safe harbor in the regulations does not include percentage compensation arrangements.

Next, the ABA believes it is especially important that the "volume or value" standard be clarified in the context of alternative payment arrangements in which physicians are paid a share of per-case cost savings, as more referrals/more procedures by the physicians may result in more savings (but may also result in lower savings). These types of payment arrangements are critical to the sorts of value-based payment approaches that CMS is actively advocating, but their legal status under the Stark Law is very unclear.

Further, some of the Stark Law exceptions prohibit the taking into account the volume or value of referrals only for Medicare DHS, whereas others expand the prohibition to also include "other business generated between the parties" (which is everything else—Medicaid, commercial pay, Medicare and Medicaid managed care, etc.). Again, this creates inconsistent guidance for providers and the risk of inconsistent enforcement actions for alleged violations. Accordingly, the ABA recommends making the prohibition on the volume or value of referrals relate only to Medicare DHS, which would better reflect the initial legislative intent behind the Stark Law (*i.e.*, protection of the Medicare Trust). Having a single, albeit more liberal, standard provides some flexibility and reduces the possibility that arrangements unwittingly violate the Stark Law because the parties are unaware that the "other business generated" standard applies. Also, to the extent that "the other business generated" standard is intended to prevent "swapping arrangements," in which favorable compensation terms may be offered on non-Medicare DHS business to induce the referrals of Medicare DHS, the AKS is available to address that, and is a more appropriate vehicle for that analysis because of the intent-based nature of AKS liability.

Finally, the ABA recommends that the statute be amended to clarify that the "volume or value" standard does not apply to personally performed services of the referring physician, even if those personally performed services are surgical procedures for which a hospital bills a facility fee. The ABA believes this recommendation is consistent with CMS's policy, but dicta from the Fourth Circuit in the *Tuomey* case[3] has caused some anxiety among hospitals and academic medical centers as to how they may properly compensate their physicians for services when those services, by their nature, result in additional revenues for the hospitals.

---

[3] United States ex rel. Drakeford v. Tuomey Healthcare Sys., Inc., 792 F.3d 364, 395 n.10 (4th Cir. 2015).

Conclusion

The Resolution herein requests that the American Bar Association urge Congress amend the Stark Law to address concerns described in this Report and provide greater clarity, consistency and fairness in the interpretation and enforcement of the statute.

The Health Law Section requests that the American Bar Association House of Delegates adopt this Resolution.

Very truly yours,

Alexandria Hien McCombs
Chair, ABA Health Law Section
August 2019

General Information Form

Submitting Entity: Health Law Section

Submitted By: Alexandria McCombs, Chair
Health Law Section

1. **Summary of Resolution(s).**
   The Resolution urges Congress to enact legislation to amend the Ethics in Patients Referrals Act of 1989, 42 U.S.C. § 1395nn (commonly known as the Stark Law), to modernize the law and encourage the adoption of value-based payment arrangements and other coordinated care arrangements that will lower costs to the Medicare program and improve the quality of services to its beneficiaries.
2. **Approval by Submitting Entity.**
   The Council of the Health Law Section approved the filing of this Resolution and Report on May 5, 2019.
3. **Has this or a similar resolution been submitted to the House or Board previously?**
   There has not been a similar resolution filed.
4. **What existing Association policies are relevant to this resolution and how would they be affected by its adoption?**
   There are no known Association policies directly relevant to this Resolution.

General Information Form *(Continued)*

5. **If this is a late report, what urgency exists which requires action at this meeting of the House?**
6. **Status of Legislation. (If applicable)**
There is no current legislation pending proposing relevant changes to the Stark Law. However, there may be legislative activity soon, as we have been informed that the Senate Finance Committee is exploring statutory changes to Stark, and both HHS's Centers for Medicare & Medicaid Services (CMS) and Office of Inspector General have recently issued Requests for Information concerning potential changes in the regulatory exceptions to the Stark Law and the Anti-Kickback Statute. Earlier this year, Congress made minor changes to the Stark Law, which it characterized as for the purpose of modernizing the law.
7. **Brief explanation regarding plans for implementation of the policy, if adopted by the House of Delegates.**
The sponsoring entities will work with the ABA Governmental Affairs Office to actively engage in federal and state legislative activities related to this issue.
8. **Cost to the Association. (Both direct and indirect costs)**
There are no known costs to the Association.
9. **Disclosure of Interest. (If applicable)**
There are no known conflicts of interest.
10. **Referrals.**
By copy of this form, the Resolution will be referred to the following entities:

Section of Administrative Law and Regulatory Practice
Section of State and Local Government Law
Section of Science and Technology Law
Law Practice Division
Law Student Division
Young Lawyers Division
Commission on Law and Aging
Commission on Disability Rights
Commission on Women in the Profession
Standing Committee on Ethics and Professional Responsibility
Standing Committee on Lawyers' Professional Liability
National Association of Bar Executives
National Bar Association Inc.
National Conference of Bar Presidents

(Continued)

General Information Form *(Continued)*

11. **Contact Name and Address Information.**
Alexandria McCombs, Chair
ABA Health Law Section

Signify Health
4055 Valley View Ln, Ste 400
Dallas, TX 75244
D: (972) 715-3800
C: (972) 533-4074
alexandriamccombs@gmail.com

Simeon Carson, Director
ABA Health Law Section
321 N. Clark St.
Chicago, IL 60654-7598
(312) 988-5824
simeon.carson@americanbar.org

12. **Contact Name and Address Information. (Who will present the report to the House? Please include name, address, telephone number, cell phone number, and e-mail address.**
William W. Horton, Delegate
ABA Health Law Section
Jones Walker LLP
420 20th Street North, Ste 1100
Birmingham, AL 35203
(205) 244-5221
whorton@joneswalker.com

Robyn S Shapiro, Delegate
Health Sciences Law Group LLC
7670 N. Port Washington Rd., Ste. 201
Fox Point, WI 53217
Ph: 414-206-2101
Fax: 414-206-2109
robyn.shapiro@healthscienceslawgroup.com

Executive Summary

1. Summary of the Resolution.

The Resolution urges Congress to enact legislation to amend the Ethics in Patients Referrals Act of 1989 (commonly known as the Stark Law) to modernize the law and encourage the adoption of value-based payment arrangements and other coordinated care arrangements that will lower costs to the Medicare program and improve the quality of services to its beneficiaries.

2. **Summary of the Issue that the Resolution Addresses.**
   The Resolution would eliminate or reduce the penalties for certain technical violations of the Stark Law that do not reasonably present a risk of fraud and abuse in the modern physician payment context, especially given the proliferation of alternative and value-based payment arrangements. The proposed legislative amendments would further simplify compliance with the Stark Law, keeping in step with other recent regulatory changes and Centers for Medicare and Medicaid Services policy initiatives towards reduction of unnecessary regulatory burdens.
3. **Please Explain How the Proposed Policy Position Will Address the Issue?**
   The Resolution would propose amendments to the existing Stark Law legislation including those that would (i) alleviate regulatory burdens associated with self-disclosure of certain Stark Law technical violations, (ii) simplify determinations of fair market value in transactions subject to the Stark Law, and (iii) eliminate certain technical issues associated with compensation "determined in a manner that takes into account the volume or value of referrals."
4. **Summary of Minority Views or Opposition Internal and/or External to the ABA Which Have Been Identified.**
   No minority views or opposition have been identified.

Index

N

O

P

T

U

V

W